Second Edition
Updated and Expanded

Canadian
Cheese

A Guide

Kathy Guidi

D0039627

FIREFLY BOOKS

A FIREFLY BOOK

Published by Firefly Books Ltd. 2014
Copyright © 2014 Firefly Books Ltd.
Text copyright © 2014 Kathy Guidi

First printing

Publisher Cataloging-in-Publication Data (U.S.)
Canadian cheese : a guide / Kathy Guidi.
Originally published as: Canadian cheese : a pocket guide, 2010.
2nd ed., updated and expanded.
[240] pages : col. photos., maps ; cm.
Includes bibliographical references and index.
Summary: A guide to Canada's artisan cheese producers and their products, as well as notes on tasting, varieties, storing and selecting Canadian cheeses.
ISBN-13: 978-1-77085-362-1 (pbk.)
1. Cheese varieties – Canada. 2. Cheesemakers – Canada. I. Title.
637.30971 dc 23   SF271.G834   2014

Library and Archives Canada Cataloguing in Publication
Guidi, Kathy, author
Canadian cheese : a guide / Kathy Guidi.
-- Second edition, updated and expanded.
Includes index.
Originally published: Toronto : McArthur, 2010.
ISBN 978-1-77085-362-1 (flexibound)
1. Cheese--Varieties--Canada. I. Title.
SF274.C2G85 2014   637'.350971   C2014 901151-2

Published in the United States by
Firefly Books (U.S.) Inc.
P.O. Box 1338, Ellicott Station
Buffalo, New York 14205

Published in Canada by
Firefly Books Ltd.
50 Staples Avenue, Unit 1
Richmond Hill, Ontario L4B 0A7

Cover and interior design: Hartley Millson
Cover photograph: Hal Roth

Printed in Canada

The publisher gratefully acknowledges the financial support for our publishing program by the Government of Canada through the Canada Book Fund as administered by the Department of Canadian Heritage.

Photos graciously provided by: Back Forty Artisan Cheese, Balderson Cheese, Quality Cheese, Best Baa Dairy, Dairy Farmers of Canada, Fromagerie La Moutonnière, Fromages CDA, Laterie Charlevoix, La Fromagerie Alexis de Portneuf, La Fromagerie Polyethnique, La Maison d'Affinage Maurice Dufour, Mariposa Dairy, Photography at MAPAQ, Plaisirs Gourmets, Salt Spring Island Cheese, Saputo Canada, Upper Canada Cheese and istockphoto © pialhovik pages 12, 27, 51, 75, 97, 146, 183, 195, unless otherwise noted.

The author is indebted to the following for permission to reprint excerpts:
Cheese and Fermented Milk Foods by Frank V. Kosikowski. Used by permission of the publisher, New England Cheesemaking Supply, see page 11
Corina Murphy, 'Luscious Immersion' Poem; corina.murphy@peelsb.com, see page 17.
My Life In France, Anchor/Random House, NY 2006, by Alex Prudhome and Julia Child, see page 45.

Contact Kathy Guidi at cheeseguidi@gmail.com

Dedication

*Dedicated to our cheesemakers, the pioneers of Canadian cheese
and to cheesemongers, who are the caretakers,
and to cheese educators, who teach the value —
together you make the Canadian cheese world renowned.*

Acknowledgments and Thanks

According to Greek mythology, Aristaios, son of Apollo and Cyrene, was sent by the gods to give the gift of cheesemaking to the Greeks. It was called "a gift of everlasting value." A truer gift there never was!

The following list of people, to whom I am sincerely grateful, is short compared to the long list in my heart. The book would not be were it not for: Firefly Books, who grabbed onto the vision of an updated edition from Ann Ledden, sales director and passionate caseophile; Hartley Millson who took on the challenge of organizing the material for visual appeal and flow; copy editors Lisa McAlpine (cheese text) and Gillian Watts; cheesemaker and teacher Debra Amrein-Boyes; forever friends Judy Chamberlain, Debbie Levy, Janet Dawson, Sydney Patterson, Connie Smith and Robin Swank for your unwavering encouragement and tasting assistance; and Hervé and Laurent Mons and Sue Sturman from Academie Opus Caseus who (inadvertently) inspired the Old and New World context of this edition.

Contents

Dairy Farmers of Canada

New in This Edition

In the first edition of this book I told you about my journey in cheese and provided a snapshot of the burgeoning cheesemaking craft in Canada. In this edition, four years later, I am honoured to expand on the cheesemakers' journey in Canadian artisan cheese, sharing more about the pioneers who create new cheeses, their inspiration and their roots, as well as passing along some new nuggets of cheese knowledge to further your appreciation of fine cheese.

There is a lot of new information in this edition. Tasting notes for 38 new cheeses have been added, and many of the cheese notes from the previous edition have been expanded. Canadian goat cheese now has its own chapter to highlight the variety in this cheese family. As well, there is a full and expanded chapter on Canadian washed rind cheese to spotlight the incredible variety and quality in what I believe will be our point of excellence in the world of cheese over time, much as Cheddar has established our legacy to date. Some of the cheeses in this edition are available only in their home provinces, but I chose to include them in an effort to support the many new artisans who make cheese their livelihood.

In this book there is a sub-theme that links New World Canadian cheese to Old World "heirloom" cheese—varieties that have been around for hundreds (if not thousands!) of years. This historical perspective fascinates me, and I believe it helps us to better appreciate our artisan cheeses and industry. The great European cheeses have influenced many of our cheesemakers in what they make. To know the history and attributes of these "model" cheeses is to understand our own. Discussed in this book are 31 traditional European cheeses presented on their own, in addition to many others offered along with the Canadian cheese that bears their name.

Pairing suggestions for beer and Canadian cheese have been added by cheese family, because enjoying these two fermented products together is becoming as popular as wine with cheese. The basic concept is to find balance between the beer and the cheese by seeking characteristics in each that complement or contrast each other, recognizing that mild cheese goes better with lighter beer while stronger-tasting cheese harmonizes with bigger-flavoured beers.

Are you curious as to what cheeses Canadian cheesemongers, cheese writers and cheese educators enjoy in their personal time? Find out in What's on Your Cheeseboard? Eleven picks of three cheeses each are slotted throughout this book. Use them as a guide for putting together your own cheeseboard as you seek new varieties to try, or simply walk in some celebrity "cheese shoes" for a night. Of course, all of the cheese picks are presented in this book.

Using the tried and true "ladder of cheese appreciation" is the best way to get to know and enjoy more cheese. In this edition, the ladder suggestions—If You Like This . . . Try This!—have been expanded within each family, starting with a European heirloom cheese as the first rung in the ladder. My advice to students is to try one new cheese a week, and ideally to cross-reference it with other cheeses tasted from that ladder group by keeping a cheese journal. There are many ways to build your own ladders; mine are simply suggestions to get you started.

To love cheese you should know something about it, and that is an ongoing learning process. Therefore, several new Cheese FAQs have been added with answers to questions I get at cheese tastings, such as why some cheese is seasonal, what calcium chloride is, what is "artisan" in cheese, Canadian cheese in competitions, and nutrition labelling on artisan cheese. Plus you'll find clearer nomenclature for *raw, unpasteurized* and *pasteurized* cheese used in the tasting discussions. Thankfully, the industry is coming together on this confusing but important issue.

Sometimes you need information fast, so this edition has an index of cheeses and topics that makes using the book easier. And websites for Canadian cheesemakers featured in the book have been added (see Appendix D) so you can get more information about your favourite makers or cheeses and follow their progress.

I hope you find this edition interesting and helpful and that it helps to provide respite from a crazy world through cheese appreciation and enjoyment—something we could do well to learn from the Europeans. Remember: slow down when eating cheese so you can savour each and every bite. Try to visualize the dairy animal grazing in the pasture, the cheesemaker gently scooping curds into the moulds, and the *affineur* turning and/or washing the cheese, waiting for it to glorify this ancient craft that expresses the best of the land and animals through a simple liquid—milk. That's truly appreciating cheese.

We all share cheese. It is a cultural icon in food that brings out our common bond as humans in the most primal and enjoyable manner. Why else would we "say cheese" when being asked to smile for a photograph?

Wishing you a lifetime of outstanding cheese experiences!
 — *Kathy*

How to Use This Book

t's no wonder customers end up buying the same old cheese, even if they want to try something new. Standing in a cheese store gazing at scads of new and unfamiliar cheeses, many with cute or foreign-sounding names, people are intimidated and fearful of appearing unknowledgeable to the cheesemonger and other customers. And unlike wine, cheese cuts are small and the labels are rarely large enough to include useful information (mandatory nutrition information and bilingual labelling rules compound the problem). As well, not every cheese can have a sign in the display, and finding a knowledgeable cheesemonger who takes the time to talk with you can be a challenge. *Canadian Cheese: A Guide* can enhance your cheese experience in the following ways:

1. Take this book with you to the store. Over the years, hundreds of caseophiles (that is, cheese lovers) have told me they take the short tasting notes from events where I speak to cheese stores so they can buy a specific cheese they enjoyed. Whether you're shopping at a supermarket, a farmers' market or a small *fromagerie*, this book is a trusty quick reference that suits the mobile, knowledge-centric foodie lifestyle.

2. Try cheese by family style. The major focus of this book is on tasting notes. Cheeses are organized alphabetically within their cheese family (fresh, soft, firm, etc.). Grouping by cheese family is a logical way to present handling, pairing and cheesemaking information. Learning about cheese this way makes cheese purchasing and understanding easier and allows you to select a new cheese similar to one you may have enjoyed previously (likely from the same family). This is like trying a new variety of apple: if you like a Red Delicious, trying a Golden Delicious, Jonagold or Gala apple isn't a huge step, but they do add variety and interest to your fruit selection.

In the world of cheese, this is called the "ladder of cheese appreciation." It doesn't matter where you start or what you prefer; what's important is to try other varieties, because it's very probable you'll enjoy a number of other cheeses that are similar in taste, texture or style to the ones you like already. To help you with the daunting challenge of what to try next, the

What's on Your Cheeseboard?

Allison Spurrell
Co-owner/Cheesemonger
Les Amis du Fromage, Vancouver, BC

Lady Jane
Alpindon
14 Arpents

ladder suggestions in this edition have been expanded. Once you get started I am sure you will want to continue the exploration on your own.

Rather than preaching in this book, I generally prefer to let you discover "truths" about cheese, with three notable exceptions: (a) freezing a cheese abuses it, rendering it suitable only for cooking at best; (b) a fresh cut of fine cheese is always better than a precut one; and (c) the best cheese is made from 100% pure, whole, real milk that has not been broken down into its individual components (these are called "modified milk ingredients" in the ingredients list).

This book is not a technical dissertation; the points made are "nutshell" explanations. Although expanded from the first edition, it still will not teach you all there is to know about cheese, nor does it feature every Canadian cheese made. It is, however, a collage of cheese information that includes notable Canadian artisan cheeses from across the country (up to mid 2013). I hope this book will spark your interest in and curiosity about cheese and prompt you to talk with your cheesemonger. There are more fine Canadian cheeses than a single cheese purveyor can realistically carry, but cheesemongers are businesspeople and they want to stock what you are interested in.

Canadian Cheese: A Guide is a handy, informative and accurate handbook that can be used often (rather than just sitting on a bookshelf or the coffee table) by both new and savvy caseophiles in discovering the great cheeses of Canada. Take it with you shopping, to restaurants, and when travelling. Check off what you taste. Write comments in the margins or on sticky notes. Use the admittedly over-simplified but, I hope, helpful phonetic pronunciations when asking for a cheese with a difficult name that you want to try. I speak *français très peu* and am often challenged when trying to remember and pronounce many of the names. Rest assured, the body language of cheese appreciation greatly compensates for any verbal language barrier that you may encounter—after all, body language is said to make up 60% of communication anyway.

3. Keep your *Guide* handy when serving cheese, so you can read about a fine Canadian cheese as you enjoy and share it with others. Names, websites and locations of cheese plants are provided so you can use the Internet to look up more information about a cheese or facility.

Most of all, I sincerely hope *Canadian Cheese: A Guide* will help you to really enjoy the experience and the pleasure of cheese.

Cheesemaking can be likened to a violinist playing his instrument. The viola has four strings but the degree of strength with which the violinist applies the bow and the knowledge of when and how to apply it, leads to either a concerto or a lullaby.

—*from* Cheese and Fermented Milk Foods, *by Frank V. Kosikowski, North American cheesemaking teacher and cofounder of the American Cheese Society*

The Ladder of Cheese Appreciation

It doesn't matter where you start or what you prefer, what's important is to try other varieties, because it's very probable you'll enjoy a number of other cheeses that are similar in taste, texture or style to the ones you like already.

The Raw Milk Question

Does raw milk make cheese better? Can raw milk cheese be made in Canada? These are loaded and popular questions! Here are the short answers: no, raw milk does not guarantee a better-quality cheese (a skilled cheesemaker is essential); and yes, raw milk cheese can be made in (and imported into) Canada, but it must be aged 60 days before being sold. That said, Quebec has a provincial rule allowing raw milk cheese to be sold after 21 days, if the *fromagerie* meets certain stiff criteria. It should be noted that, since 2010, the term *raw milk* can refer only to the use of milk (or curd) that has not been heated above 40°C, the approximate body temperature of the cow. While only a few Quebec cheese plants are actually doing it, this book includes Pont Blanc (page 61) and Gaulois de Portneuf (page 58), both of which are Quebec "less than 60 days old" raw milk cheeses.

The 60-day rule came into effect in 1949 and was designed primarily to combat pathogens found in fluid (drinking) milk that were causing disease in humans. After 60 days, harmful bacteria that may be present in raw milk are generally deemed to be dead. However, new data suggests that harmful pathogens may be introduced after pasteurization, at any time during the cheesemaking, packaging and distribution processes. And cheese made with raw milk may actually be able to fight off post-cheesemaking bacteria better than pasteurized milk cheese, because of the good bacteria that remain in unpasteurized cheese. If you look at the incidence of sickness or death from cheese (raw or pasteurized) compared to other foods (produce, processed meat, processed foods), cheese has a pretty clean record. That being said, the Canadian Food Inspection Agency (CFIA) warns people who may have compromised immune systems—pregnant women, elderly people, people with HIV/AIDS or people who have recently had chemotherapy—to avoid raw milk cheese, particularly the soft ripened varieties.

As long as there is freedom of choice for the consumer regarding the purchase of raw milk cheese, I am okay with the 60-day ruling . . . for now. To understand the issue, you must understand the history. Pasteurization of milk was only discovered in the late 1800s and was applied to cheese in the early 1900s. For thousands of years the world ate raw milk cheese. The big issue then and now is sanitation, whether on the farm, in the cheesemaking plant or during distribution (which includes retail stores and restaurants).

North American cheesemaking is still in its infancy compared to Europe. Our cheese industry started growing when pasteurization was seen as the panacea for safe cross-country and global cheese distribution. North American cheese processors embraced pasteurization (with a few exceptions, such as Canadian aged Cheddar) as a way to grow their business. In Europe, raw milk cheeses were, and still are, sold in local or regional areas within a country. People buy and consume cheese every day or every few days. The pattern for cheese selling and consumption is vastly different there.

It was the rebirth of local and artisan cheese production that caused the raw milk cheese issue to surface in North America. Change, especially when it might involve public safety, comes slowly, but consumer demand will continue to grow. Collaboration, rather than appeals to emotion, is the answer. A strong cooperative effort between the CFIA and cheesemakers to set standards for raw milk cheese-making practices is needed. Clear documentation (sometimes called a HACCP, or Hazard Analysis Critical Control Point, Risk Reduction Plan), starting on the farm where the milk was produced, continuing though the cheesemaking and ripening process, and right until the cheese leaves the door of the plant or ripening facility, will add credibility to raw milk cheesemaking. Raw milk cheese production has never been mainstream in North America. Records that show bacteria levels and practices at all the stages of production are a necessary evil to resolve the concern over raw milk cheese safety, as well as to benchmark best practices within a cheese facility. The good news is that this work is underway in Quebec, at the "less than 60 days" approved cheese plants, and with the Raw Milk Coalition founded in the United States.

That I appreciate and enjoy the complexity of a well-made raw milk cheese goes without saying. More importantly, I believe that raw milk cheese is more nutritious, by virtue of the enzymes and micronutrients that remain alive in the milk, and therefore in the cheese. However, I take my hat off to the expert cheesemakers who take "dead" pasteurized milk and add layers of flavour into the cheese by using intricate combinations of bacteria cultures and their expertise. Making superior cheese from pasteurized milk can and is being done, as you will see when you try cheeses made by Fritz Kaiser, The Farm House Natural Cheeses, Éco-Délices, Domaine Féodal, Salt Spring Island, or Fromagerie Le Détour, to name just a few.

Cheese FAQ: What is the difference between pasteurized, thermized and raw milk?

Pasteurized Milk

During pasteurization, milk is heated to 63°–75°C for 15 seconds to destroy various pathogenic bacteria and make the milk more uniform in quality for cheesemaking. The downside? This destroys the naturally occurring organisms that enhance cheese flavour and nutritional attributes.

Thermized (Unpasteurized) Milk

Thermized milk, also referred to as *thermalized, heat-treated* or *non-pasteurized* milk, undergoes a treatment by which it is heated to 54°–57°C prior to cheesemaking for 2 to 16 seconds, allowing some of the flavour-contributing enzymes normally destroyed in pasteurization to survive, as well as many potential pathogens. Cheese made with thermized milk is generally more flavourful than cheese made with pasteurized milk, but it is regarded by regulators as raw milk and thus these cheeses must be aged 60 days before they can be sold.

Raw Milk

Raw milk comes directly from the animal and is heated prior to cheesemaking only enough to initiate fermentation (30°–40°C). The use of raw milk is not a quality guarantee but potentially results in a cheese with a more complex, layered and lingering flavour. The cheese must be aged a minimum of 60 days before selling, to comply with regulations regarding raw milk cheese. There is an exception to this rule in Quebec (see page 12).

How to Eat Cheese (Like a Pro)

How to eat cheese is one of the first things I share with people in classes and tastings, because in North America cheese is often a convenient snack that we gulp down rather than a food to be treasured and savoured, as it is in Europe. Of all the cheese information I pass along, how to eat cheese is what most people respond to—they say it changes forever the way they enjoy cheese! Yet the process is so simple. You don't require special knowledge or tools, and the tasting notes in this book will help you build your cheese description vocabulary. Simply take a moment with each bite to use the gift of your senses:

Sight — Note the cheese's shape and size, the colour of the curd or paste, its rind (colour, type and condition) and the body of the cheese (is it dense or does it have holes?).

Touch — Go ahead and touch it. Is the cheese very supple (soft), moderately so (semi-soft) or firm? Is the rind waxy, velvety (like the fabric), sticky, hard or sandy?

Aroma — Smell the cheese, both paste and rind. Does the aroma entice or repel? Is it a familiar smell, like nuts, milk, mushrooms, grass, or wildflowers?

Flavour — Place a bite of cheese on your tongue. Roll it around and press it to the roof of your mouth (rather than chewing it) to generate saliva. Allow it to linger a few seconds. Take note of the predominant and subtle qualities. Notice whether the primary flavours (sweet, sour, salty and bitter) are balanced. Notice the secondary or lingering flavours (these often mirror the cheese's aroma but in many cheeses are generally more subtle). Be descriptive: is the cheese simple (some are supposed to be) or are its flavours complex, layered and lingering?

Mouth Feel — Again this is about touch. Is the texture in your mouth creamy, smooth, grainy, buttery, silky, or chalky?

Imagination — I consider this the sixth sense. When eating the cheese, does it take you places (back to the farm, a special trip or occasion, the countryside)? Does it excite you or bore you? Is it ecstasy (five stars), mediocre (three stars) or disappointing (one star, if any)?

What's on Your Cheeseboard?

Andrew and
Jonah Benton
Owners
Benton Brothers Fine Cheese,
Vancouver, BC

Lady Jane
Alpindon
Grey Owl

In summary, suck on your cheese the way you would a fine Belgian or Swiss chocolate. Everyone knows how to do that and almost everyone does it automatically with chocolate—mmm! (Incidentally, I'll have my chocolate with a lovely lactic ripened goat cheese on the side, an amazing combination introduced to me by one of my early students. Thanks, Connie!)

Immerse yourself in this art
as if you were trying a new and exotic fruit.
Peel away the skin of your inhibitions
and bite into the bold colours and abstract designs.

Let its whimsy roll around in your mouth,
its multi-layered flavours permeate your tongue
and its lushness spill like juice down your chin.

And once you've savoured it
SHARE your experience with a good friend
so they, too, may relish something new and exotic.

— Luscious Immersion,
by Corina Murphy, Guelph, ON

Fresh
Unripened
Cheese 1

All You Need to Know about Fresh Unripened Cheese

Typically, high moisture content—up to 80% of the milky whey is left in the cheese—makes fresh cheese soft and often spreadable. It's called fresh because it receives little or no aging. Fresh cheese is a close reflection of the milk from which it's made. Thus, fresh cheeses will have milky, mild flavours and are great "beginner" cheeses despite the fact that they can be quite complex. The downside is that their shelf life is quite short and they must be used promptly.

Most cheese is made from just four ingredients: milk, bacterial culture, salt and enzymes. "Starter culture" is the bacteria added to milk at the beginning of cheesemaking to ferment it by raising the lactic acid level. This promotes souring of the milk and helps with curdling. Almost every cheese type (with the exception of a few fresh styles mentioned below) uses a second bacterial culture that contributes to the final flavour and look of the cheese. Salt adds flavour, suppresses spoilage bacteria and aids in ripening of the cheese. Enzymes assist in fermentation and help eliminate whey (the watery liquid exuded from the curds).

A few simple fresh cheeses do not use bacterial culture, relying instead on a coagulant—lemon juice, vinegar or a microbial enzyme—and a specific recipe technique to determine the style of cheese. Minimal salt (if any) is used because it would cause more whey to leave the cheese and make it firmer. Although fresh cheeses can be made from any dairy animal milk, in Canada they are most often made from cow milk. It is a special treat to find a goat or a sheepmilk ricotta or a simple brebis (sheep milk "chèvre" style). Flavourful buffalo milk fresh cheeses are also becoming more common.

Little Miss Muffet Sat on Her Tuffet, Eating Her Curds* and Whey

Cheese is a concentrated form of milk. It is created during fermentation, the controlled acidification of milk. Fermentation is the complex process of souring milk by adding a starter culture early in the cheesemaking process, in order to convert lactose (milk sugar) to lactic acid, which causes the milk to curdle. The curd becomes what we know as cheese. Bread, wine and cheese are all fermented products. The French call them the "holy trinity of food" because they go so well together.

* probably cottage cheese

Cheese FAQ: Do you make cheese at home?

I started to make fresh ethnic cheese with students as part of a culinary class unit on cheese, and because I love to cook with ethnic cheese. Although my cheese turned out fine, the time, patience and cleanup required for cheesemaking presents a challenge to my going beyond making simple fresh cheese. I have to say, however, that cheesemaking is a uniquely nurturing and fulfilling experience that helps you appreciate the craftsmanship involved. If you want to make cheese at home, I strongly recommend using recipes from a book by Debra Amrein-Boyes, *200 Easy Homemade Cheese Recipes* (Toronto: Robert Rose, 2013). Debra is the European-trained cheesemaker at The Farm House Natural Cheeses in British Columbia. She told me that you have to use more culture in small batches, but otherwise the recipe and process are pretty much the same as what she does at her farmstead plant.

Heirloom Cheese: The Fresh Unripened Family

The most ancient heirloom cheeses are in this family, with ancient literature confirming cheese production as far back as 4000 BCE. In the Iliad and the Odyssey, Homer recounted how cheese sustained the men in the Trojan Horse and also described the giant Polyphemus making a cheese similar to feta. Later, in Roman times, the historian Pliny the Elder recorded detailed recipes for cheese enjoyed by emperors during faraway conquering expeditions. In fact, so longed for were the ancient cheeses, it wasn't unusual for a cheesemaker to be brought back as a captive to reproduce the cheese for the Romans.

Simple yet often elegant, fresh cheese was typically created out of a need to add variety to the daily diet, and to preserve milk in months when there was more milk than could be used by the farm family. In fact, "cottage cheese" refers to the cheese made by farm women in the cottage home.

Cheese is a simple, pure, nutritious food that has been used for basic sustenance throughout recorded history. In Canada (mostly outside Quebec), cheese is generally considered an accessory to food, something you use in a recipe or, worse yet, an indulgence. In Europe cheese is food, a main source of protein. The definition of *farmstead* is milk that goes from animal to vat in a few hours. Traditional recipes add starter culture to the raw milk at night so that while the milk is resting, acidification occurs and cheesemaking can begin. This is the true meaning of slow fermentation.

Today we generally regard the heirloom cheeses in this family as "ethnic cheese," and they generally have the same name as in their country of origin. Canadian caseophiles are just discovering the amazing legacy that immigrants have brought with them. We are blessed with "made in Canada"

Cottage cheese

Bocconcini

diversity right on our doorstep. From Italy come ricotta, fresh mozzarella, bocconcini, stracchino, tuma; from France, chèvre (fromage frais); from Portugal, St. John's, in both cow and goat versions; from India, paneer made from milk or whey and milk; from Latin America, queso fresco, queso panela and queso duro; from Greece, feta (actually a fresh cheese preserved in brine); from Scandinavia, juusto (bread cheese); from Cyprus, Haloumi; from Lebanon, Nabulsi and Twist; as well as Labneh from countries of the eastern Mediterranean.

I am a big fan of artisan fresh cheese for a number of reasons besides their rich cultural history. Fresh cheeses are inexpensive (pound by pound) compared to ripened cheese, because their technique is simpler and they require minimum if any ripening. But more important is that they add authenticity to traditional and popular recipes from other lands that just can't be achieved with a New World cheese substitute. Plus, when you use the authentic cheese in an "ethnic" recipe, every bite takes you on a mini trip to some faraway destination.

Heirloom Cheese in This Family
Barrel-Aged Feta (Greece)

The most famous traditional Greek cheese dates back to Homeric times. Authentic PDO (see page 29) feta requires the cheese be made in Greece according to traditional methods, from local raw or pasteurized sheep milk and/or up to 30% local goat milk, naturally drained with no pressing, and aged a minimum of 60 days in a wooden barrel. Greek feta is rich and salty with a slightly sour tang, crumbly yet moist. Feta means "slice," which describes the chunks that go into the barrel containing the brine of salted whey. Buy and store it in brine (1 tbsp/15 mL salt per 1 cup/250 mL water) to preserve the quality if your feta isn't in brine when you buy it.

Handling and Storing Fresh Unripened Cheese

Keep fresh unripened cheeses cold (35° to 39°F/2° to 4ºC) at all times. Unopened fresh cheese will last from a few days to several weeks, depending on the packaging. Once opened, it is important to use a fresh cheese within three to five days, as it may get noticeably sour after that. Keep the cheese sealed in a plastic container so it doesn't lose moisture and to prevent absorption of unwanted flavours or aromas. Mass-produced (industrial) cream cheese contains stabilizers and/or gums to increase the cheese's shelf life, while some fresh cheese is wrapped in special packaging that extends the life of the cheese. However, it's still best to use these cheeses within three to five days of opening them.

Fresh Unripened Cheese with Canadian Wine and Beer

Dry to fruity white wines such as Vidal, Chenin Blanc and Pinot Grigio work well with the mild, milky flavours of fresh cheeses. Flavoured fresh cheese may need a more robust wine, depending on the seasoning; for example, fresh cheese flavoured with peppercorns, rosemary or spices may be better suited to a medium-bodied red such as Merlot.

Beer and cheese are both fermented products and thus pair well together. The effervescence of beer cleanses and refreshes the palate much like the acidity in wine. From delicate light golden ales to dark and robust brews, there's a profusion of beer shades and flavours to choose from. Light, crisp beers with delicate and refreshing flavours work well with fresh cheese, especially if the cheese is served au naturel or with just a dollop of olive oil and cracked pepper. If the cheese is flavoured you can ramp up the beer to complement the cheese spicing. That said, as with any other pairings, remember that your taste preference is always your best guide.

Ladder of Cheese Appreciation: Fresh Unripened Cheese

If you like the heirloom cheese on the bottom rung of the Ladder, you will probably enjoy the Canadian cheese on the other rungs. It's not that they necessarily taste the same but that they have similar characteristics, such as texture and body. The flavours may be more or less similar depending on the age of the cheese at the time you taste it.

Quark

Stracchino

Burrata

Fresh Mozzarella

St. John's Cow or Goat

Ricotta

Tasting Notes

This Canadian-made assortment will get you started on expanding your appreciation of fresh cheese. The "ethnic" varieties can be found in larger cities, especially if that specific cultural group is part of the demographics. You may have to visit a culturally specific store to find some of them, but there you will also find other ingredients to accompany the cheese. Remember, if you like any one of these cheeses, it is likely you'll like others in the fresh cheese family.

Feta

Ewenity Feta
Best Baa Dairy
Fergus, ON
made from raw or
pasteurized sheep milk.

Feta Moutonnière
Fromagerie La Moutonnière
Sainte-Hélène-de-Chester, QC
from a fromagerie that also
makes sheep feta in cold-pressed
olive oil with fines herbs.

Tiras Goat Feta
Tiras Dairies
Camrose, AB
from a cheesemaker that
specializes in production of
Greek-style cheese.

Feta is the quintessential warm-weather cheese. I tend to add small chunks (not crumbs, as they lose their identity) to just about anything that needs a white splash of salty, cheesy zest. Preference for this native Greek cheese is highly personal, with some folks liking it creamy and sharp with a lemony tang, and others preferring it crumbly and salty. To get my attention, it has to be made from sheep or goat milk, sold in whey-based brine, and full-flavoured enough to stand on its own merit with olives and bread.

Canadian Cheese

A Cheese by Any Other Name

A 2005 European Union ruling mandated that in the EU the name feta can be used only for cheese made in Greece from the milk of sheep or goats pastured in Greece. As a result, in Europe there is a lot of faux feta called "white cheese," and a lot of consumers wondering what happened to traditional feta. Sadly, even in Greece, restaurants are switching from the original to less expensive "white cheese" (from cow milk) while calling it feta. If you travel to Greece, be sure to ask for real PDO feta. There is a world of difference between it and the cheaper substitute!

•••

The flavour of fresh mozzarella is mild, like sweet milk. The body should be tender and not too elastic, a sign of overworking by machines. "Fruit of the milk" or *fior di latte* (pronounced *fee-or dee LA-tay*) in Italian, is another way to describe this fresh, soft cow milk cheese. Its warm, delicate curd is hand pulled (a signature of the pasta filata cheese category, see page 70) to keep it tender and to develop its characteristic elastic texture. Fior di latte is the original version of mozzarella used for pizza in Italy; it refers to any mozzarella made from cow milk. This is a different mozzarella cheese than the ripened semi-soft mozzarella we are familiar

•••••••••••••••••••••••

Fresh Mozzarella

Santa Lucia
International Cheese
Toronto, ON

Bella Casara
Quality Cheese
Vaughan, ON

Mozzarina Mediterraneo
Saputo
Saint-Laurent, QC

with in Canada (although it too is *pasta filata*, or "pulled curd").

Fresh mozzarella is usually tennis to softball size. Twisting the curd into various knots and shapes produces cheeses with names such as bocconcini ("morsels"), Treccia ("braid") and Noddini. Fior di latte and bocconcini are the cornerstone cheeses for a Caprese salad with fresh tomatoes and basil.

Fresh Mozzarella from Buffalo Milk

Bella Casara
Quality Cheese
Vaughan, ON

Natural Pastures Cheese
Courtenay, BC

Fans of the Italian *di bufala* (pronounced *dee-boo-fa-la*) version of mozzarella can be true to locavore goals with fresh soft buffalo milk mozzarella from  Ontario or British Columbia. It has the same springy, soft texture and delicate yet rich, milky flavour as Italian *bufala* mozzarella at a fraction of the price and eco-footprint. Buffalo milk has a considerably higher fat and protein content than cow milk. I find buffalo milk fresh mozzarella more tender and rich than fresh mozzarella from cow milk. Bella Casara also offers a bocconcini size of fresh buffalo mozzarella.

Cheese FAQ: What animal milks are used for cheese?

Approximately 98% of the cheese in Canada is made from cow milk. Outside North America, goat, sheep and water buffalo dominate the cheesemilk animals. A full 15% of the world's cheesemilk comes from water buffalo; in fact it is the milk that predominates in Southeast Asia. In other parts of the world, cheese is also made from horse, camel, yak and reindeer milk.

Bill Bickle

This spreadable cream cheese–style cheese is pure temptation, mirroring fresh cream cheese but with less milk-fat (cream cheese typically has 26–30% MF, Grey Rush 21% MF). Handcrafted from low-temperature pasteurized cow milk (to retain the fresh milk flavour), the curd is cautiously drained until just enough whey is retained to keep the cheese spreadable. The body is light and creamy and the taste clean, with a mildly tangy sour cream taste and just a hint of salt, without any of the additives or preservatives so often found in cream cheeses and spreads. The plain version is a fine base for adding your own flavours (such as honey, chutney or jam), or try the hot chile pepper or herbed varieties.

Grey Rush

Primeridge Pure
Markdale, ON

Tasting Notes

Guernsey Girl

Upper Canada Cheese
Jordan, ON

If cheese is the ultimate convenience food, Guernsey Girl leads the pack with a nutritious take on traditional Scandinavian-style juusto, a semi-soft fresh cheese. In its package, this Guernsey cow milk cheese looks like a de-crusted mini loaf of egg bread (holes and all), which is why it's sometimes called "bread cheese." It's best served warm, when the flavour magically changes from kind of bland to buttery and nut-like. Simply warm 1/2-inch (1 cm) slices of the cheese in a skillet on both sides, until bubbly, soft and golden-coloured. The cheese becomes flowing, with a thin, crispy crust, when warm, and it squeaks when chewed. Think of it as grilled cheese without the bread (yum!). You can serve it with multigrain bread or my favourite way—on top of cut-up kale or rapini that's been braised with onions and garlic.

Haloumi

Fromagerie Polyethnique
Saint-Robert, QC

Haloumi (sometimes called Halloom) is a semi-soft unripened cheese with a sweet milk flavour and a salty finish. Traditionally made from sheep or goat milk, in Canada it is made from pasteurized cow milk; sometimes it has fresh chopped mint added to the curd or sandwiched within the folds of the cheese. At the factory the fresh curd is baked to give it typical non-melting characteristics, and then it is put into a salt brine. The traditional cheese of Cyprus, this fresh

cheese is often eaten in kebab form (un-grilled) with watermelon. In Canada, Haloumi has grown in popularity as a grilling cheese. Polyethnique's products are certified halal under the Phoenicia Group's Cedar brand.

Labneh

Fromagerie Polyethnique
Saint-Robert, QC

In countries of the eastern Mediterranean, this soft, creamy white cheese with a slightly lemony taste is made from yogurt. It is a staple food in many countries in the world. Labneh may have different names depending on geography, for example, Chakka in India, Skyr in Iceland, Mastou in Iraq and Sakoulas in Greece. To serve, spread some labneh on a plate, drizzle with olive oil and serve with flatbread and olives.

Nabulsi

Fromagerie Polyethnique
Saint-Robert, QC

You'll find Nabulsi an interesting semi-soft pasteurized cow milk cheese that is sweet but salty. It is usually scented with exotic spices such as kolongi seeds and mahalab. Nabulsi is native to the city of Nablus, located north of Jerusalem. It is also available in Twist, a firm cheese braided into a twisted format. After loosening the cheese mass by soaking it in water for a few minutes, Twist is eaten by tearing thin strings off the braid.

Tasting Notes

Paneer

Asli Paneer
Local Dairy
Ingersoll, ON

A popular ingredient in many Indian recipes, this soft unripened cheese is made with fresh cow milk and vinegar if it is regular *Asli Tazza Swad Mazedar Paneer*, or with milk, whey and vinegar if it is *Malai Paneer*, a lower-fat version. Both are available in 350-gram bricks and are made from time-honoured family recipes. Paneer is not something you want to serve as a table cheese, because it is a bit bland and rubbery, but that said, it has a fresh, clean milk taste. Preparing it the traditional way, by frying it briefly till browned, adds colour and makes the cheese very supple. While warm, the cheese is squeaky to the bite, like a fresh cheese curd. As it cools it gets firm again, so eat it warm and keep it warm for those who want seconds. It will soften again if reheating is needed.

For 20 years Asli cheese and dairy products have maintained a rich, authentic Indian flavour by using milk from in and around Oxford County. Local Dairy's line of Indian dairy products under the Asli brand also includes Shudh Ghee (clarified butter for cooking), Dahi (authentic Indian yogurt with live probiotic cultures), Makhni (whipped cultured butter for baking, cooking and spreading) and Khoya (a condensed milk–based confectionary ingredient used to enrich Indian desserts).

Quark

The word *quark* is German for "curd." Misunderstood in North America, delicious quark is a very soft fresh unripened cheese usually made with cow milk. Originating in Germany and central Europe, it is sold in a tub because it has a body resembling Greek yogurt or ricotta. Quark is naturally low in fat, with an airy, super-creamy texture and the flavours of cultured milk and salt, with a refreshingly sour finish. Use as a spread (seasoned with honey or preserves), an ingredient in sauces (instead of cream) or as a substitute for cream cheese with sliced cucumbers, smoked salmon and dill on bagels or rye bread.

**The Farm House
Natural Cheeses**
Agassiz, BC

**Rocky Mountain Quark
Foothills Creamery**
Didsbury, AB

Armadale Farm Dairy
Roachville, NB

Queso

Queso means "cheese" in Spanish and is pronounced *kay-so*. For several years it has been a fast-growing category of cheese consumption, accommodating not only Latin Americans living in Canada but also cooks who want to use authentic cheese in their Mexican and South American menus. Recipes use different styles of fresh queso at every meal, with liberal amounts crumbled on enchiladas, empanadas, burritos, tacos, soups and other hot foods. Once you've used authentic queso in your Tex-Mex and Latin recipes, you'll never go back to Monterey Jack, mozzarella, or Cheddar

Grandpa's Dairy Produce
London, ON

Latin Foods
Calgary, AB

Dairy Farmers of Canada

as substitutes because the texture and flavour are just too inauthentic.

Grandpa's Dairy Produce, London, ON
Grandpa's is one of two companies in Canada that are in the lead in terms of queso quality and variety. The firm produces these classic versions:

Queso Panela is a somewhat bland pure white cooking and snacking cheese made from pasteurized cow milk. It adds colour contrast, texture and nutrition to Latin and Tex-Mex foods. It also provides a rich depth to Latin breads and pastries, and it is traditional to add very small cubes of the cheese to dark hot chocolate—this has much the same effect as adding marshmallows, except it's healthier and more interesting.

Queso Puro Mexicano is a cornerstone of Latin cooking that falls into the category of fresh cheese with grilling properties: it softens but doesn't melt when warmed, taking on a unique elastic texture and clean milky taste. The bite and characteristic neutral flavour is absolutely right for Latin cuisine.

Latin Foods, Calgary, AB
Raphael Chavez, of Latin Foods in Calgary, was a farmer who made cheese from his dairy cows' milk in his native Venezuela. He moved to Alberta a few years ago and since 2010 has been living his dream of making Latin American

cheese from 100% Canadian cow milk. The cheese is made at the Alberta Food Processing Development Centre in Leduc, Alberta, which is an Agrivalue Processing Business Incubator program.

Queso Fresco ("fresh white cheese") is a traditional cheese with a slightly salty taste and a smooth, soft texture that doesn't melt. Cube it or crumble over salads and soups or in refried beans. The cheese will take on the flavour of the surrounding food and spices.

Dairy Farmers of Canada

Queso Paisa is a semi-soft cheese that is lower in fat and salt than queso fresco. It also has a higher melting point than other cheese, which makes it suitable for frying and grilling.

Queso Duro is the third major group of Latin cheese. These are grating-style cheeses with names such as Cotija, seco and duro blando. They are high-salt hard cheeses with a dry, crumbly texture that are grated over hot foods, meats and soup.

Ricotta is traditionally made from whey boiled with a bit of vinegar, lemon juice or citric acid until curds form and rise to the top (the word *ricotta* means "twice cooked"). Adding a little milk to the whey makes the cheese richer and smoother in taste. Ricotta is a great substitute for cream cheese, with more calcium and protein and less fat. Expect

Ricotta

Bella Casara Ricotta
Quality Cheese
Vaughan, ON

Tasting Notes

Santa Lucia Ricotta
International Cheese
Toronto, ON

Dairy Farmers of Canada

St. John's Cow Fresh Cheese

Portuguese Cheese Company
Toronto, ON

ricotta to have a fresh, clean, milky aroma and taste and a smooth texture that melts on your tongue. It is both light and rich—a real comfort food!

Ricotta is wonderful on toast with a smear of jam or topped with fresh fruit as a dessert. In Toronto you can buy these ricottas at the factory store, just hours old and packed in whey (the closest thing to enjoying it in Italy). Bella Casara Ricotta was the first fresh cheese ever to win Grand Champion at the Canadian Cheese Grand Prix, which shows that among cheese experts, a well-made fresh cheese can have all the sophistication of an aged cheese. The traditional packaging (a small basket holds the cheese) allows the whey to drain into the cup and makes a lovely pattern on the cheese. Remember, once you open any ricotta package, you should use it within three days for the best flavour.

This authentic Portuguese fresh cheese, made from pasteurized cow milk, is a daily staple in the Portuguese community. It has been produced in Toronto for more than 40 years but most people are unfamiliar with it. The curd has a custard-like texture and a sweet milk taste and aroma, and it is free of animal rennet. It's marvellous with fresh fruit for breakfast or a great substitute for bocconcini in a Caprese salad. The

Portuguese serve it with a *pimenta moula* (red pimiento) sauce. St. John's is a traditional fresh cheese, not packaged for extended shelf life, so it lasts only two weeks. The liquid in the package is whey, which is emitted as the cheese matures.

Stracchino

Bella Casara
Quality Cheese
Vaughan, ON

I really love stracchino (pronounced *strah-kee-no*) cheese. Its sensual honey-like texture, thin rind and sweet/lactic milkiness send tingles through my body. I am so glad it's now made in Ontario under the Bella Casara label. Serve it for breakfast on whole wheat toast or use it to top a pizza, as they do in Italy. I'm known to just cut open the top rind and dive in with a spoon—stracchino is my personal substitute for ice cream!

Tuma

International Cheese
Toronto, ON

You must try this traditional cheese of Piedmont, Italy. Tuma (pronounced *TOOM-a*) is a fresh, creamy table cheese that's eaten as is or, particularly at holiday time, breaded and lightly fried. Bacterial culture gives the cheese its special flavour, while moulding the curds in a small basket adds interest to the cheese's appearance.

Soft Ripened Cheese 2

Dairy Farmers of Canada

All You Need to Know about Soft Ripened Cheese

The fresh unripened cheeses in the previous chapter are soft largely because of the amount of moisture they contain (up to 80%). The cheeses in this chapter are still soft—their moisture content is 50 to 60%—but they're also classified as "ripened" (as are all the cheeses from this point on).

"Ripening" describes the period following cheesemaking when fresh moulded curd becomes the unique cheese it was destined to be. Ripening is sometimes called "curing" or "aging," but whatever name is used, it is always done under precise temperature, humidity and air flow conditions. During ripening, proteins change and interact with the culture bacteria which was added to the milk to develop the specific qualities of an individual cheese variety, such as flavour, texture and type of rind.

The soft ripened cheese family includes three types:
• soft cheeses with a white bloomy rind
• soft cheeses with an orangey-brown moist washed rind (discussed in chapter 4)
• soft "mixed rind" cheeses: a combination of bloomy and washed (also in chapter 4)

Each of the soft ripened cheese types ripens from the outside (the rind) towards the centre. The changes in soft ripened cheese occur quickly, over a period of a few weeks. The cheese starts off mild and somewhat firm, then progresses to very supple (or, for some, even runny or unctuous). Flavour becomes more intense as the cheese ages. Increased suppleness is most likely to occur when the cheese is made using traditional methods. Soft ripened cheese made from stabilized (ultrafiltered) milk remains somewhat firm, although it can still be buttery in texture.

Particular moulds or bacteria (or both) grow on the outside surface of these cheeses to form the rind (known as the "flower" or crust). The rind contributes to flavour, body and texture development during ripening and in the finished cheese. You may see the phrase "exterior surface or mould ripened" on the label or in the description of a cheese. They mean the same thing. *Penicillium candidum* is the most common bloomy rind bacteria culture, and *Penicillium geotrichum* is also popular.

High moisture content and their delicate rind cause these cheeses to ripen quickly. The larger 3-kilogram wheels of soft ripened cheese ripen more slowly than smaller 500-gram wheels and are often more gentle in flavour. I prefer to buy small wheels because the rind remains uncut until I use it, so the cheese ripens in a more natural state. Also, I find that smaller wheels deliver truer flavour. Before buying a small wheel, press the cheese gently to determine its state of ripeness; then smell it to check for the appropriate aromas. There is an old French adage that says a perfectly ripe soft ripened cheese should feel as supple as your eyeball (caution: close your eyelid first!).

Brie and Camembert cheeses are immensely popular, appreciated for their creamy mouth feel and snowy white bloomy rind, and perhaps because they have the cachet of legendary French classics. The downside of their popularity is that they're often produced in industrial quantities,

What's on Your Cheeseboard?

Roxanne Keeping
Cheesemonger
All the Best Fine Foods, Toronto, ON

Le Pizy
Sabot de Blanchette
14 Arpents

using milk that has been standardized through ultrafiltration. Mass production and double-crème butterfat have changed many classic Old World cheeses into somewhat bland, tough-rinded versions of the originals, produced with shelf life in mind rather than taste, so they never fully ripen. In fact, I believe this is why Canadians have a preoccupation with baking, stuffing or smothering bloomy rind cheeses with savoury jellies.

Milkfat (MF) plays an important role in the texture and flavour of all cheese, but this is particularly true for bloomy rinds. In fact there are three distinct styles of bloomy rind cheese created just by having different fat levels:

- Traditional (or regular) Brie/Camembert contains the least fat (about 22% MF) and has the most authentic flavour.
- Double-crème—created decades ago by the French, who added additional milkfat to traditional Brie to seduce North American taste buds, which found traditional Brie too piquant—has approximately 28% MF.

Julia Child's Experience with a Parisian *Fromagère*

The drill was to wait patiently in line until it was your turn, and then give your order clearly and succinctly. Madame was a whiz at judging the ripeness of the cheese. If you asked for a Camembert, she would cock an eyebrow and ask at what time you wished to serve it: would you be eating it for lunch today, or at dinner tonight, or would you be enjoying it a few days hence? Once you had answered, she'd open several boxes, press each cheese intently with her thumbs, take a big sniff and—voila!— she'd hand you just the right one. I marvelled at her ability to calibrate a cheese's readiness down to the hour, and would even order cheese when I didn't need it just to watch her in action. I never knew her to be wrong.

> — from *My Life in France*, by Julia Child and Alex Prud'homme

• Triple-crème Brie/Camembert has pasteurized cream added to the cheesemilk and contains about 38% MF. This is the decadent dessert cheese that often resembles cheesecake or cultured butter in texture and flavour.

All three types of these bloomy rind cheeses have a predominant mushroom or truffle aroma and taste that originates from the rind.

The percentages of milkfat (MF) noted above are unique to Canada, where milkfat is measured as a percentage of the fat in the total product. In the United States and the European Union, milkfat is measured as a percentage of "dry matter," after all the moisture is removed. The fat percentage on an EU cheese label will make it look as if the cheese has almost twice as much fat as the Canadian version. However, the Canadian cheese isn't lower in milkfat, it's just measured differently.

Cheese FAQ: Should I eat the rind?

Eating the rind is a matter of choice. In a nicely ripened cheese the rind adds to the flavour, and I recommend eating it. In a cheese that is less than *à point* (perfect), the rind can detract from enjoyment of the cheese and should not be eaten. There is no golden rule. We all have different levels of sensitivity to flavour. I have had students who prefer an ammonia-tasting advanced-age Brie and others who can barely tolerate even the gentlest of rind flavours. If you have reservations about eating the rind of a cheese, taste the paste (the interior) first. If you like it, chances are you'll enjoy the rind too; so with the next bite, try them together. Remember, some people eat the skin of an apple or a potato and some don't. Neither is right or wrong. Just enjoy your cheese.

Cheese FAQ: What is artisan cheese?

The word *artisan* is the latest overused word in marketing, just as *natural*, *gourmet* and *premium* have been. The focus of this book is on artisan cheese. (Note: the word is *artisan*, not *artisanal*. *Artisan* is easier to say and the latter gets confused with water wells.) Although some large companies produce high-quality artisan-style cheese (a few are in this book), they are not artisans by definition. Artisan cheesemakers have hands-on involvement with all aspects of production (and often sales, marketing and distribution as well); they know firsthand where their cheesemilk comes from and what the animals eat and their state of well-being. Also, being an artisan means the cheese is probably made in small batches and by hand, with plenty of ladling, curd cutting and pressing, turning, brushing and washing of wheels—along with expertise in traditional methods of cheese production. In my mind, being an artisan cheesemaker in the 21st century also means giving attention to safe milk-handling practices and participation at some level in a risk-reduction program geared to ensure food safety, as well as the reputation for making cheese of consistent quality.

Heirloom Cheese: The Soft Ripened Family

Many of our Canadian artisan cheeses are modelled after Old World recipes. Some were cloned intentionally to represent the attributes and taste of the original, while others started off with the model and built on it to fashion a Canadian (New World) original. We can be proud of both approaches. When is an heirloom cheese a model? The answer may be found in another question: when do we like a painting, a decorating style or a dish eaten in a restaurant enough to copy it, but with a flair of our own that is distinct from the original?

I asked an (artisan) cheesemaker from the Italian Slow Food Presidia if he minded someone trying to copy his cheese. He replied that it was no problem if the new version was a good representation of his cheese, adding something along the lines of "The world needs more good cheese." He then added that it should have a different name so there would be no confusion between his cheese and the new one. In fact, he said, it was a compliment to have someone try to copy his work and it motivated him to stay on top of his quality, to remain the gold standard. I asked other EU cheesemakers the same question and got similar answers. There's no doubt that European artisan cheesemakers are passionate about their craft, and happy to mentor and pass on the centuries of knowledge behind their cheese to fellow artisans in the New World.

Heirloom Cheese in This Family

Brillat-Savarin (France)

One of the earliest triple-crèmes, Brillat was created by Henri Androuët in the 1930s in honour of the renowned 18th-century French epicure and gastronome Jean Anthelme

Brillat-Savarin, who wrote *The Physiology of Taste*. Expect rich but mild buttery and sweet nut flavours from this cow milk cheese, along with a slight tang from the bloomy rind. One of the easiest ways to encourage a new caseophile is through a triple-crème! Similar varieties include **Saint-André**, **Boursualt** and **Délice de Bourgogne**.

Brin d'Amour (Corsica, France)

Soft, mild and aromatic—the name "breath of love" was enough to entice me to try this lovely sheep milk cheese. It has an herbal crust of rosemary and savory punctuated by juniper berries on top. As it ages, the herbs permeate the cheese paste and the cheese firms up. Say *bran dah-moor*. **Fleur de Maquis** is similar.

Chaource (France)

The roots of this small bloomy rind cow milk cheese can be traced back to the 14th century. In 1513 the cheese was named after a town in Champagne and given to an important official. This PDO double-crème bloomy rind, with tinges of red as it ripens, has an almost fluffy paste that is buttery smooth with a creamy centre and runny around the edges. Rich nutty, fruity and mushroom flavours abound. No wonder so many cheesemakers used it as a model for their creations. The name is pronounced *shah-oorse*.

Robiola (Italy)

Even the name sounds decadent and rich as it rolls off your tongue. This group of small mixed cow, goat and/or sheep milk cheeses hail from Lombardy and Piedmont. The name refers to the style of cheese, of which there are many examples, including several coated in ash or wrapped in leaves (even cabbage leaves). All are soft and oozing when perfectly ripe, with a thin, delicate rind and silky interior texture. The aroma is milky, with pleasant sour cream tartness and slight vegetal and sea salt flavour notes that coat the palate. Late summer/early fall is when this cheese is at its best. Say *roh-bee-OH-lah*.

Saint-Marcellin (France)

Easily identifiable by the brown crock it comes in (used to help the cheese hold its shape), this soft cow-milk cheese is satiny in texture and spoonable when ripe. It has a most delicate clotted-cream, buttery, nutty taste. In France it is often served alongside arugula or baby mixed greens, dressed with just a drizzle of olive oil and a lemon wedge on the side. It was originally made from goat milk. King Louis XI introduced Saint-Marcellin to his court in the 15th century, in honour of some local people who had fed him bread and cheese when he was lost in the woods as a young prince. Say *san mahr-se-lahn*. **Saint-Felicien** is similar.

What's on Your Cheeseboard?

Debbie Levy
Cheese Educator
Savour This, Toronto, ON

Five Brothers
Avonlea Clothbound Cheddar
Bleu d'Élizabeth

Handling and Storing Soft Ripened Cheese

The rinds on these cheeses need to "breathe" or they will suffocate and develop a very bitter taste. Try to buy small wheels packed at the factory or pieces freshly cut from a large wheel and/or within three days of having been wrapped in plastic. If the cut is plastic-wrapped, remove the plastic and rewrap loosely in waxed or parchment paper when you get home. Placing wrapped pieces in a plastic container helps control the aroma, but remember to keep the air in

Canadian Cheese in Competition

In the previous edition of this book, I added a comment in the tasting notes if a cheese had won top of category or better in a major competition, and I had intended to do this again. However, the idea was discarded because there are nearly as many winners as there are cheeses in this book—it seemed a bit overwhelming! The fact is, hundreds of Canadian cheese have won top honours in competitions all over the world, and there are hundreds of these competitions. Entering a competition is useful to cheesemakers for the expert feedback the judges can provide on both the technical and aesthetic qualities of a cheese, as well as supplying ideas on how to improve features in a cheese. Winning a competition is a great assist in marketing the product and keeping the attribute bar that drove the achievement high. Congratulations to all the award-winning Canadian cheesemakers. Keep up the good work!

by not "burping" the container, and be sure the container is about three times larger than the piece of cheese.

Full wheels of any soft ripened cheese (at home or in stores or restaurants) should be turned over every day or two to expose the rind on the underside to air. All cheese, and especially the fresh and soft varieties, should be purchased and used like produce. Enjoy these delicate lovelies within a week of purchase. Cheese is a living food; to be at its best, it should be consumed within a short period of time.

Soft Ripened Cheese with Canadian Wine and Beer

While sparkling wines are my personal favourite with this category of cheese, a full-bodied oaky Chardonnay, off-dry Riesling or fruity Gewürztraminer is also an excellent choice. The combo of sweetness and acidity in icewines, late-harvest wines and hard ciders makes them wonderful choices with these cheeses too.

The carbonation in beer cleanses the palate by lifting the soft cheese off your tongue. Try a light wheat-style beer such as Berliner Weisse Ale for contrast, or a sharp, dry style such as a lambic. Belgian beers, with their low-hopped fruitiness and yeasty profile, partner well with mould-ripened soft cheese, and stout with a triple-crème is quite amazing.

Ladder of Cheese Appreciation: Soft Ripened Cheese

If you like the heirloom cheese on the bottom rung of the ladder, it is likely that you will enjoy the Canadian cheese on the other rungs. It's not that they necessarily taste the same, but they have similar characteristics such as texture and body. The flavours may be more or less similar, depending on the age of the cheese at the time you taste it.

| Lady Jane |
| Brebette |
| Pizy |
| Pont Blanc |
| Figaro |
| French Saint-Marcellin, Italian Robiolla or French Chaource |

Tasting Notes

Albert's Leap

Quality Cheese
Vaughan, ON

Rich and full-flavoured, with the character and complexity of a French farmstead Brie, this double-crème bloomy rind benefits from the use of both *candidum* and *geotrichum* bacteria, as well as the essential French technique of gentle curd-handling. The rind is tender and velvety while the taste is of earth and mushroom, with no bitterness. Albert Borgo, the cheesemaker, feels that cheese has as much character as its maker. Available in 200-gram and 1-kilogram wheels, the small size will ripen faster and develop more flavour, although the larger size is no slouch!

Ash-Ripened Camembert

Moonstruck Organic Cheese
Salt Spring Island, BC

Purebred Jersey cows are the cornerstone of this organically certified farmstead operation where cheese is made in small batches. Sisters Julia and Susan Grace work to keep the cows happy and healthy so that the milk is sweet and fragrant. They are dedicated to simple cheesemaking methods that produce cheese of fine texture and deep flavour. Climate changes on the island, from extremely dry to very wet, result in specific styles of cheese being made in a season. Spring milk is best for cheese that requires aging. Winter milk is heavy with both protein and butterfat, perfect for wonderful creamy soft and semi-soft cheese styles. The plant is provincially licensed, meaning their cheese can be sold only in British Columbia.

Grey to black ash beautifully mottles the normally white bloomy rind and causes it to ripen more slowly. The paste has a musty aroma and flavour notes of earthy mushroom and butter. Ash-Ripened Camembert is a pasteurized cheese, ready to eat in two weeks, but proteolysis (that's the nice runny texture) is really established in a month. The Grace sisters feel this cheese is ready for the compost pile at 60 days—except for those who are not faint of heart.

Dairy Farmers of Canada

Bliss

Monforte Dairy
Stratford, ON

Triple-crème cheese is always luscious and addictive, but you haven't experienced anything until you've tasted Bliss. This is a soft bloomy rind made with Ontario sheep milk enriched with cow cream, yet still considered a double-crème (28% MF) by soft cheese fat standards. The typical snowy white thin rind leads to a paste that, when ripe (at room temperature), has a mouth-filling, substantial finish and a balance between the sweet taste of cultured butter and tangy sour cream, with a hint of salt.

Tasting Notes

Brebette

Best Baa Dairy
Fergus, ON

I didn't feel this cheese was quite ready to include in my 2010 book. However, time has served Brebette well, with its gorgeous brain-patterned *geotrichum* rind lending vegetal flavours to this small, soft boule of creamy pasteurized sheep milk cheese. Below the tender, thin rind the smooth paste is often edged with a runny cream line. The flavour is delicate and fresh in the interior and more cultured and aromatic at the outer edges. This is a sophisticated, rich and sensuous cheese that changes character in a matter of days—from wonderful to outstanding—as the paste matures and lingers longer on the palate. Enjoy this cheese within a week of buying it. As with other small but great cheeses, the *à point* period can be relatively short.

Most artisan cheesemakers are both the marketing and sales managers for their cheese. Merchandising at farmers' markets is just as important as in a retail setting because it communicates images of quality and premium value. Kudos go to Best Baa for its display strategy at Toronto farmers' markets, where the cheese is displayed on ice (packs) covered with tea towels. There are information signs about each cheese, and the soft lactic and bloomy rinds are open (not wrapped in plastic), exposed to the air they love, and packaged to take home in plastic tubs to protect them from squishing. Firmer cheeses are nicely wrapped in plastic with the name on the label.

This fresh, soft, slightly aged sheep milk cheese is gently wrapped in a wine-soaked maple leaf. As delicious as it is beautiful, with a silky paste and range of tastes from lactic to hazelnut, it achieves a perfect balance of cheese and wine notes via that macerated leaf. Twenty years ago, sheep farmer Lucille Giroux imported the first flock of dairy sheep from Europe and was the first person to make and sell sheep milk cheese in Quebec. La Moutonnière has its federal licence now and distribution outside Quebec.

Cabanon

Fromagerie La Moutonnière
Sainte-Hélène-de-Chester, QC

Hal Trussel

Pronounced *sahn-dray day pray*, this soft bloomy rind Brie-style cheese has a thin layer of maplewood ash in the centre. Made from pasteurized cow milk, this handcrafted cheese is permeated with distinctive flavours and floral aromas originating from the land.

Cendré des Prés

Fromagerie Domaine
Féodal, Berthierville, QC

Discerning Quality in a Cendré

The ash line through the centre of a cheese is called *cendre* (French for "ash"). My cheese-maker-judge partner at a cheese competition explained the technical difficulty involved in getting the layers of curd to knit after sprinkling ash on the first layer. If not done at precisely the right moment of curd development, the layers will separate when cut, which defeats the decorative purpose of the ash line.

Dairy Farmers of Canada

Tasting Notes

Comox Brie

Natural Pastures Cheese
Courtenay, BC

This superb bloomy rind cheese exhibits gentle flavours, a creamy, buttery texture, and the traditional delicate notes of mushroom. You can count on its consistency after this cheesemaker's many years of honing the recipe into its distinctive yet classic style.

Evanturel

Thornloe Cheese
Thornloe, ON

On the surface this looks like ordinary Brie, but one cut into the buttery paste reveals a thread of colour from natural vegetable ash that, though largely decorative, adds a vegetal note. Its delicate truffle flavour, with a balanced salt and cultured-cream taste and a tender, thin bloomy rind, demonstrates the craftsmanship that is used to make this cheese.

Farm House Camembert

The Farm House Natural Cheeses
Agassiz, BC

This farmstead Camembert is made on a family dairy farm from fresh pasteurized cow milk. The farm has what is called "wandering barns"—the cows are not tied up in the barn and can decide if they want to be inside or out.

The smooth, buttery interior of this lovely Camembert clone is encased in a white bloomy crust. The aroma is musty, like mushrooms, with a rustic pronounced vegetal taste that suggests complex bacteria are used. The plant still has only a provincial licence, meaning you can find Farm House Natural Cheeses only in British Columbia, but thankfully getting a federal licence is in the works.

Figaro

Glengarry Fine Cheese
Lancaster, ON

Dairy Farmers of Canada

This tiny square of soft, mould (surface) ripened cow milk cheese delivers cheesecake ecstasy on the tongue with its yeasty aroma; rich, creamy texture; thin skin of a rind; and sweet-to-tangy cultured milk and vegetal notes. Some people recommend it for use as a spread, but in my opinion it is far too elegant and flavourful to be mashed and masked by a croissant or bagel. Make it a habit to savour the cheese and then the bread. My favourite foods to team with this cheese are roasted fennel, broccoli or asparagus (when in season); Medjool dates also offer a delicious texture and flavour contrast. Although fashioned after French Chaource, Figaro is also similar to the soft, lactic surface-ripened cheese Robiola (Italy) and Saint-Marcellin (France).

....

Fleurmier

Laiterie Charlevoix
Baie-Saint-Paul, QC

Fleurmier (pronounced *flerr-mi-eh*) is an elegant double-crème Camembert encased in a velvety, tender bloomy rind. The body is supple and creamy, with a delectable cream and mushroom aroma and flavour notes. Charlevoix is a particularly beautiful region of Quebec, with a strong dairy heritage despite its long winters.

La Galette

Fromagerie de la Table Ronde
Sainte-Sophie, QC

This is an elegant soft washed rind made from pasteurized organic cow milk. It's a double-crème but has the luxurious rich texture of a triple-crème. A flowery tender rind protects the melt-in-your-mouth pale yellow paste; its clean rich and buttery flavours end with a touch of sea salt to cleanse the palate on the finish.

Gaulois de Portneuf

Ferme Ducrêt
Saint-Basile-de-Portneuf, QC

Using raw Jersey cow milk, Ferme Ducrêt is one of the rare Quebec cheese plants with permission to sell raw milk cheese matured for less than 60 days. To maintain this licence the factory follows very strict rules, including daily analysis of each batch of cheese and keeping a detailed log containing required bacteria information on the milk and cheese until it leaves the plant. The farm has only 20 cows, which are fed grass and hay from the farm. Rudy Ducrêt keeps a strict eye on each step in the creation of his cheese, from soil quality to animal well-being to cheesemaking and curing. His task is to help prove that raw milk cheese production can be safe, especially under the guidance of a dedicated artisan.

Gaulois has a beautiful soft bloomy rind composed of several moulds with colours of beige, white and bluish grey—all of which give the cheese a unique character. When it's young, expect a creamy fresh and deliciously floral cheese experience; when older, there are some meaty animal notes. The luxurious ripe avocado textured paste and deep yellow colour are a trademark of soft Jersey cow milk cheese. The complex simplicity of these well-con-structed flavours is a sign of a great artisan.

. . . .

Patterned after Chaource, an aristocrat in the legions of French cheese, Lady Jane has a dense, creamy cheesecake texture. It is made from pasteurized cow milk and offers a buttery tri-ple-crème richness inside a thin surface ripened rind which seems lightly citrus, and a lovely complement to the clean, cultured tang of the paste, which melts on the tongue. This cheese gets more supple with age until it is an oozy bliss.

The Farm House cheese plant and farm are located in the lush Fraser Valley, where cows and goats graze on field grass in season and eat organic hay from the farmland in winter. The cows are Guernsey, Brown Swiss and a few Jerseys, ancient breeds whose milk has a higher percentage of the beta carotene and protein desired in cheesemaking than other breeds of cow. Although the farm is not certified organic, no pesticides, hormones or antibiotics are used.

. . . .

Lady Jane

**The Farm House
Natural Cheeses**
Agassiz, BC

Tasting Notes

Marquis de Témiscouata

Fromagerie Le Détour
Notre-Dame-du-Lac, QC

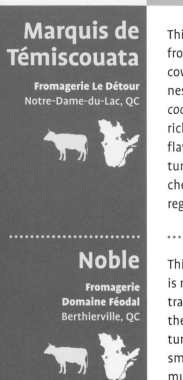

This soft bloomy rind cheese is made from the thermized milk of local Jersey cows, which accounts for its extra richness. Pronounced *mar-kee deh tay-miss-coo-wata*, it is handcrafted to deliver rich buttery to mushroomy aroma and flavours and an unctuous, velvety texture. "Marquis" is the nickname of the cheesemaker and Témiscouata is the region where the factory is located.

Noble

Fromagerie Domaine Féodal
Berthierville, QC

This fine handcrafted Brie-style cheese is made with pasteurized cow milk. The traditional bloomy rind is tender and the body supple, with a velvety texture. Enjoy the musty aroma, luscious smoothness and delicate taste of fresh mushrooms and almonds. The name is pronounced *nob-leh*.

Dairy Farmers of Canada

Piacere

Monforte Dairy
Stratford, ON

Pronounced *pee-ah-chair-ay* (the Italian word for "pleasure"), this marvellously seductive cheese lives up to its name! The surface ripened rich sheep milk cheese is slathered with rosemary, savoury chile pepper and juniper berries to create a most unique visual and flavour experience that unfolds as it melts in your mouth. A first-rate replica of French Fleur de Marquis, with Ontario distinction!

Pizy

Fromagerie La Suisse Normande
Saint-Roch-de-L'Achigan, QC

It is always fascinating to me how complex the milky lactic bacteria flavours of butter and mushroom can be. This soft, thin disc of bloomy rinded pasteurized cow milk cheese has a rich butter yellow exterior and is nothing short of addictive. There is mastery in the specific bacteria combination used and in the gentle handcrafting. Say *pee-zee*.

Pont Blanc

Au Gré Des Champs
Saint-Jean-sur-Richelieu, QC

Only a farmstead operation using organic raw cow milk could create such a masterpiece of flavour! Hand ladled into small moulds in traditional French style, the paste softens in just a few weeks and the rind might exhibit a dot or two of blue on the surface. Au Gré Des Champs creation, Pont Blanc, is one of the few raw milk cheeses allowed to be sold under 60 days old in Canada (see page 12 for an explanation).

Tasting Notes

It's the colour of straw, with a silky, mouth-coating texture; the aroma and flavour are delicately lactic and grassy with a light finish of sea salt. But be advised, this very exquisite soft ripened cheese is greatly influenced by the aromatic plants and wildflowers the cows forage on in the pasture, so the flavour will vary from one season to the next. Reminiscent of Saint-Marcellin, Pont Blanc can be bought only in Quebec because Au Gré Des Champs is a provincially licensed plant. Should you snag a piece of this delicacy, enjoy it ASAP for it only has about two weeks in its life left after you buy it.

Ramembert

Best Baa Dairy
Fergus, ON

"Elegant" best describes this miniature bloomy Camembert made with pasteurized sheep milk (note the clever play on the name of the cheese). It's best at room temperature, when the cheese is quite supple and rich flavours of mushroom and clotted cream coat the palate. These precious cheeses are sold in clear plastic tubs—a simple way to protect them from getting squished. (Perhaps my biggest pet peeve when buying soft cheese is that cheesemongers don't think to protect these fragile and often costly creatures.) Tubs allow the cheese to continue ripening nicely without being wrapped. Lift the lid and turn the cheese over in the container every other day to continue the maturation. Ramembert is also available as *Raw Milk Ramembert*, the cheese Elisabeth Bzikot, cheesemaker at Best Baa, is most proud of. It has bigger, more complex flavours, including hints of piquant reminiscent of blue cheese, than its pasteurized cousin, and is aged the required 60 days.

Riopelle (pronounced *ree-oh-pell*) is an exquisite unpasteurized cow milk tri-ple-crème in a bloomy rind with melt-in-your-mouth texture, and flavours of cultured butter, mushroom, and clotted cream. It's named for Québec painter Jean Paul Riopelle who lived in the town, Isle-aux-Grues, where the cheese is made and painted the picture for the label. For each wheel of cheese sold, one dollar goes to the Île-aux-Grues Youth Foundation, a trust devoted to advancing the higher education of young art students.

Riopelle

Fromagerie Île-aux-Grues
Isle-aux-Grues, QC

Dairy Farmers of Canada

Tasting Notes

Sheep in the Meadow

Best Baa Dairy
Fergus, ON

When animals graze in the pasture, there's no telling what they might get into! The herbes de Provence under the bloomy rind of this delicate, soft and luxurious pasteurized sheep milk cheese suggest that it could be wild rosemary and thyme. It's a very lovely combination that compliments earthy mushroom from the *Penicillium candidum* culture. Both the cheese and the herbs shine.

Soeur-Angèle

Fromagerie Fritz Kaiser
Noyan, QC

A blend of fresh pasteurized goat and cow milk with a dash of cream gives this tender double-crème bloomy rind a distinctive, slightly tart flavour. Ultra-creamy with delicate notes of mushroom and citrus, its name is pronounced *serr-on-jel*. It is named after a loving nun in the area (*soeur* is French for "sister"), who loves cheese and is an "angel" to children. A portion of the proceeds goes to Dignité Jeunesse, a local children's charity.

Nutrition Labelling on Artisan Cheese

Nutritional value is possibly the last reason a person buys an artisan cheese. Yet every precut piece of cheese bears a large printed label with this information. What makes matters worse, if you line up cheese nutrition labels and read them, the information is the same within a cheese family and has only minor differences  across cheese families. Nutrition labelling is extremely useful where it will influence a purchase decision—for instance, at a fast-food restaurant, where a person might change their decision from burger and fries to salad with dressing on the side; or with produce, so people can compare the nutrition specifics of various fruits and veggies as they shop. But people who want a piece of Riopelle are not going to change their minds and buy Avonlea Clothbound Cheddar for the difference in nutrition, any more than nutrition labelling on a bottle of wine would stop people from purchasing it.

Nutrition labels are as large as a 150-gram cut of cheese (the average size, or smaller). Together with the product label, it hides the cheese entirely and makes for unattractive merchandising. And they cost cheese companies money for something they know is a worthless consumer message, compared to a label that communicates product attributes. There are three options that I can see: supermarket cheesemongers can join forces to get the regulation changed, based on its ineffectiveness for artisan cheese; artisan cheese can be sold fresh-cut where it is now sold precut; or caseophiles can buy their cheese cut to order from cheesemongers, where a nutrition label is not required.

Dairy Farmers of Canada

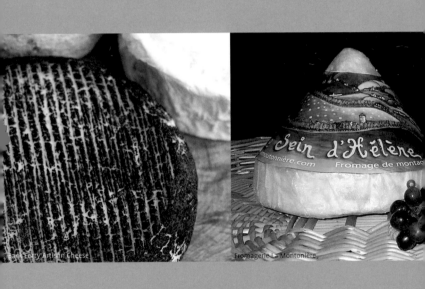

Baek Ferry Artisan Cheese

Fromagerie La Montonière

Semi-soft /
Semi-firm
Cheese 3

Dairy Farmers of Canada

All You Need To Know about Semi-soft / Semi-firm Cheese

Small changes in the cheesemaking process make big differences in the resulting cheese—mild or bold flavours, open or dense body, smooth or crumbly texture. The semi-soft family is perhaps the most diverse in flavour, and they're larger cheeses than the soft group because they have less moisture and a consequently a longer life. They are referred to as semi-firm when the cheese leans towards being firm rather than semi-soft. Either term is okay.

Common characteristics of semi-soft/semi-firm cheeses include:

- they contain 40 to 60% moisture, less than soft cheeses;
- ripening occurs from the interior of the cheese towards the outside, earning them the description "interior ripened"; and
- rennet becomes more important as an ingredient, because it expels whey and creates a firmer cheese.

Semi-soft/semi-firm ripened cheeses can get quite bitter after six to eight months, and they also get softer with age. Use them promptly if they are to be sliced or shredded, to avoid getting a gooey mess on your utensils.

Specific curd treatment during semi-soft cheesemaking depends on the style of the cheese. In general the curd is lightly cut, well stirred and possibly rinsed with hot water before it is placed in moulds—a big difference from soft cheeses, where gentle cutting and as little curd-jostling as possible is the rule. Once the cheese is in its mould, it

Cheese FAQ: What is rennet?

Rennet is the traditional enzyme that helps to expel the liquid whey during cheesemaking. It is extracted from the fourth stomach chamber of a calf. The term "rennet-free" on a cheese label means that either microbial or vegetable enzyme was used instead of animal rennet. This is of particular value for dietary regimens—for instance, Muslim or vegan—that do not allow certain animal substances, if any, in food products. Microbial enzyme, a biotechnology product that performs like natural rennet, has gained wide acceptance among some cheesemakers.

The natural animal enzyme rennet produces a better cheese, however, with a sweeter, more pliable curd, while assisting the fermentation process. It is unfortunately two to three times more expensive than the modern non-animal alternatives. While the cost of rennet is high and often it precludes vegetarians from enjoying a cheese, I must say that the majority of the fine ripened cheeses in this book use pure rennet in their recipes, as it is irreplaceable for superb curd development.

is turned frequently, with the weight of the curd pressing more whey from the cheese.

Some of the milder semi-soft cheeses are carriers for herbs, spices or—as the cheese competitions call it—"particulate matter." The common-sense rule for flavoured cheese is to start with a high-quality cheese and add high-quality flavouring. However, this category has been inundated over the years with mediocrity and redundancy in the type and quality of both cheese and flavouring. I believe that market saturation with flavoured cheese was part of the downfall of the Ontario cheese industry in the 1980s. Innovation

Cheese FAQ:
What is calcium chloride?

While milk, salt, culture and enzymes are the primary ingredients in cheese, calcium chloride is often used to boost calcium ion properties in milk that has been pasteurized or homogenized, in order to shorten coagulation time and improve curd firmness. Almost all the calcium chloride used goes out with the whey, but it has to be part of the ingredient statement in Canada if it is used.

Dairy Farmers of Canada

waned and processors lost money as they competed against each other with more and more of the same. It's a different story today, with new flavours emerging such as wasabi, chocolate and curry, to name a few.

Within the semi-soft moisture category are many pasta filata cheeses. *Pasta filata* is Italian for "stretched [or pulled] curd." The technique of stretching cheese curd while it is still warm, mechanically or by hand, develops an elastic, string-like characteristic that allows it to be made into a variety of shapes. Mozzarella, provolone, scamorza, bocconcini, fior di latte and burrata are all pasta filata cheeses.

Subtle heat and curing techniques applied during cheese-making allow pasta filata cheeses to appear in three families: fresh soft (e.g., fresh mozzarella and Italian cheeses sold in light brine liquid), semi-soft ripened (e.g. regular "pizza mozzarella") and firm ripened (e.g., aged provolone). The stretching technique is generally used only for Italian and a few Middle Eastern–style cheeses such as Halloumi and Nabulsi.

Heirloom Cheese: The Semi-soft/Semi-firm Family

The United Kingdom and Canada are at a similar juncture in some ways. In the U.K., the Second World War destroyed animals and factories, cheesemakers died and recipes were lost. It took decades to bring cheesemaking back, and actually, cheesemakers don't always know if their recipe is the original. They only know where their milk comes from and that the cheese is handcrafted using traditional methods. Technical assistance ("go to") support for traditional farmstead recipes is weak, especially if there is a problem. This situation has made it extra important for cheesemakers to truly understand their milk and to be aware of every moment in the cheesemaking process. Great artisans are a testimony to that last statement!

Canada has a key advantage compared to European artisans. Our artisan cheesemaking Industry is being spawned by young people who have chosen the life of a cheesemaker as a career, some after several family generations in dairy farming; others start with dairy farming and then move into cheesemaking when the finances are sound. In Europe, succession is a big concern. Some cheeses face extinction because there is no one to continue making them! The challenge there is to make rural life attractive to young people and the business of cheesemaking viable economically. It is interesting to remember that once upon a time, hundreds or even thousands of years ago, European artisans were the pioneers of cheesemaking. The tables have turned. Will our cheeses be the heirlooms of the future?

Heirloom Cheese in This Family

Boerenkaas (Netherlands)

With its roots back in the sixth century, Dutch Gouda, or Boerenkaas, was popular in England by the 13th century.

Discerning Quality in Mozzarella

The degree of stretch varies from mozzarella to mozzarella. Some are barely stretched and may actually be a stirred-curd rather than a true pulled-curd cheese. "Block mozzarella," as they are called, are generally lower in price. Easy to identify, they're cut from a block and thus have squared edges. They often contain modified milk ingredients and you won't be able to "string" or peel them into thin strips.

A well-crafted pasta filata mozzarella is made from fresh milk. It is stringable when cold, with a supple, elastic body that forms characteristic thin strands of golden brown cheese when heated. It is worth the extra cost over block mozzarella. As you might expect, full-fat mozzarella delivers a richer taste than part-skim mozzarella.

Women generally made the cheese because men tended to the animals. Today premium Gouda-style farmer's cheese is still handmade from raw milk on farms in the Netherlands, where it is cooked and pressed to remove whey and to encourage development of a sweeter flavour as it ages. Boerenkaas (say *boor-en-kahss*) comes aged from six months to seven years. At one year it is golden in colour and smooth and dense in texture, with subtle caramel notes. As it ages the flavours become more concentrated and the colour becomes ochre; after two or three years a smell like whisky and a taste like butterscotch predominate—sounds a bit like Aged Farmhouse from Natural Pastures.

Havarti (Denmark)

While most everyone knows Havarti cheese, few know that it is named after a 19th-century Danish farmhouse, Havartigaard, which was the home of Hanne Nielsen. She travelled

Canadian Cheese Standards

Technology advances have had a real impact on traditional cheesemaking. Cheese can be made from milk combined with milk solids such as whey, buttermilk, butter, butter oil, whey butter, whey cream, whey protein concentrates, milk protein concentrates and other milk solids rather than whole, fresh, real milk. These other ingredients show up on the label as "milk ingredients" or "modified milk ingredients" and are found mostly in industrial (large-batch) cheeses as opposed to handcrafted artisan styles.

Many countries have standards for cheese and other products to assist the consumer in identifying the product by name. The Canadian Food Inspection Agency updated the standards for all cheese sold in Canada late in 2008, setting minimum percentages for the amount of whole, real milk (that is, not broken down into components) used in different types of cheese while allowing the use of some milk ingredients in order to support new technology. Standards for aged Cheddar were also established (see page 148).

An easy way to determine if a cheese is made with 100% Canadian milk, especially at the dairy case, is to look for the Dairy Farmers of Canada "Blue Cow Logo." This marketing program uses the logo to indicate that a cheese is made with 100% Canadian cow milk and/or cow milk modified milk ingredients that are from 100% Canadian milk. Initiated in 2011, the program is voluntary (some artisan cow milk cheesemakers do not participate, and goat and sheep milk cheeses are excluded).

Photo provided by Dairy Farmers of Canada

all through Europe learning all she could about cheese-making, then came back to create Havarti. It was dubbed the "Danish Tilsit," although it is milder in both aroma and flavour.

Handling and Storing Semi-soft/Semi-firm Cheese

It couldn't be simpler. Keep the air out by wrapping the cheese in plastic wrap or self-sealing bags (with the air squeezed out) to keep the cheese from going mouldy and/or drying out. Most semi-soft/semi-firm cheeses have a best-before date of six to eight months, but at home you should use the cheese within a week or two of opening it.

Semi-soft/Semi-firm Cheese with Canadian Wine and Beer

Wine pairing is easy for semi-soft/semi-firm cheese without flavouring. Look to full-bodied whites and oaky Chardonnays that lend acidity to cut through the creamy texture of these cheeses. Light floral whites, rosés or even a fruity Merlot will also work if the cheese has some age on it. If the cheese is flavoured, pick your wine based on the spice. Wasabi, fenugreek or curry will go better with crisp whites, whereas peppercorn or truffle might require a mellow red.

What's on Your Cheeseboard?

Vanessa Simmons
Cheese Sommelier
Savvy Company, Ottawa, ON

Figaro
Le Pizy
Lindsay Bandaged Cheddar

Over the years I have worked at various wine events tasting Canadian cheese with European wines. Finding a good pairing is often difficult, because European wines tend to overpower Canadian cheese. New World wines, however, team up favourably with all the families of Canadian cheese. Both the white and red wines appear to have the right level of weight, even though the wine region may be hundreds of kilometres away from where the cheese was made.

Beer lends itself nicely to semi-soft/semi-firm cheeses, but they prefer lighter beers such as lagers. Hoppy beers are very compatible with cheeses that have grassy, fruity tastes, while sour beers contrast the creamy texture with an interplay of acidity.

Ladder of Cheese Appreciation: Semi-soft/ Semi-firm Cheese

If you like the heirloom cheese on the bottom rung of the ladder, it is likely that you will enjoy the Canadian cheese on the other rungs. It's not that they necessarily taste the same, but they have similar characteristics such as texture and body. The flavours may be more or less similar, depending on the age of the cheese at the time you taste it.

Nostralla
Frère Jacques
São Miguel
Boerenkaas
Butter Cheese (Le Polichinel)
Danish Havarti

Tasting Notes

Aged Havarti

Golden Ears Cheesecrafters
Maple Ridge, BC

This family operation opened in 2011. Sisters Jenna (the cheesemaker) and Emma (marketing and sales) Davison make a variety of Jersey cow milk cheese using milk from their uncle's dairy farm, next door to the factory. The cheese processing facility is a backdrop to the popular country store, restaurant and cooking class–centre staffed by their mom. Untraditional in approach, all the semi-soft and firm cheeses at Golden Ears are made in Gouda wheel moulds, including the aged Havarti, which has a lacy, open body and is slightly firmer with 12 to 18 months of age. The initial taste is a sour tang followed by a pleasant nuttiness, somewhat reminiscent of a young Swiss.

Boerenkaas

Natural Pastures Cheese
Courtenay, BC

The name is Dutch for "farmer's cheese" and is pronounced *boor-en-kahs*. This semi-firm smooth, rich-bodied cheese has the fragrant aroma of sweet milk and seasonal herbal and grassy flavours that capture the salad of greens enjoyed by cows pastured on Heritage Dairy Farms in the Comox Valley. Many of the cows are Ayrshires.

Bonnechere

Back Forty Artisan Cheese
Lanark, ON

The rugged Bonnechere (pronounced *bonn-share*) River and its mysterious caves are landmarks of the Ottawa Valley, where this cheese is made. A distinctive mahogany brown textured pattern on the rind of this raw sheep milk cheese is the result of lightly char- ring the cheese exterior over an open flame before aging. While charring is a traditional custom of Scandinavian cheesemakers, this recipe is actually based on a French torched cheese named Fromage de Vache Brûlé from the Basque/Pyrenees region. The end result is a deliciously toasty flavour with just a hint of smoke, contrasting with a lively fruit taste (light pineapple) and a luxurious semi-firm texture after four months of age.

Back Forty Artisan Cheese

Tasting Notes

Burrata

Quality Cheese
Vaughan, ON

Sensual and unique, the name of this small, pear-shaped pasta filata cheese means "butter" in Italian. The exterior is always fresh full-fat mozzarella, which hides a luscious centre that may be sweet cream with small fresh mozzarella curd, rich Mascarpone, or freshly churned butter. In any case, the centre oozes out gently when the fist-sized mass of cheese is cut open. No matter what is inside, after just a few bites I guarantee you'll want to know the secret of how it got in there.

Masterfully handcrafted and traditionally made only for holidays, the popularity of this cheese has prompted year-round availability. At Quality Cheese, the art of making Italian cheeses like burrata have been handed down from the Borgo family's great-grandfather, who made it and other Italian specialty cheeses in Asiago, Italy.

Quality Cheese

Chocolate Cheese Fudge

Pine River Cheese and Butter Co-op
Ripley, ON

What could be better than cheese with dark chocolate in every morsel?! This innovative product from a farmer/ cheese co-op that has been in business since 1885 is actually a cold-pack cheese food (which is a long way of saying how it is made). Havarti cheese is chopped up in a food processor and mixed with other ingredients (in this case, dark cocoa) until soft and smooth enough that it can be moulded. Although considered a processed cheese, Cheese Fudge is uncooked and must be refrigerated. Incredible paired with Cabernet Franc Icewine!

Flavoured Semi-soft Cheese

Bothwell Cheese
New Bothwell, MB

- Black Truffle Cheese
- Madagascar Green Peppercorn Cheese

Flavoured cheeses are not usually my preference, but these varieties use just the right level of high-quality spicing in a basic creamy stirred curd–style cheese, thus making them exotic and perfect for enjoying *au naturel* or as a recipe ingredient. One is delightfully seasoned with earthy Italian black summer truffles, while the other is infused with mildly spicy green peppercorns from Madagascar.

Tasting Notes

Frère Jacques

Abbaye Saint-Benoît
Saint-Benoît-du-Lac, QC

Abbeye Saint-Benoît

The look of this squatty, wheel-shaped cheese is distinctive, with an orangey natural rind and plenty of medium-sized Swiss "eyes" (holes). Mild yet distinctive, with a sweet-to-nutty taste, the cheese is a popular favourite, especially with children. In the United States this cheese would be called a "Baby Swiss" because of both its size and its semi-firm body. Made by monks at the abbey, the name and logo on the cheese label refer to the famous children's song about a sleeping monk. When you mention the name of this cheese to people, they always begin singing the song. Talk about a memorable cheese name!

Nostralla

Kootenay Alpine Cheese
Creston, BC

This semi-firm, natural rind, organic cheese is made with raw milk from the Harris family's single herd of cows. The name Nostralla means "of this place," suggesting that although the cheese emulates Italian Fontina (traditionally made in the Alps), it is unique to the Kootenay region. It has a supple, creamy texture and mildly earthy to sharp and fruity flavours after a minimum of 60 days cave aging.

Polichinel (Butter Cheese)

Laiterie Charlefoux
Sorel-Tracy, QC

When you crave an uncomplicated, crowd-pleasing cheese, look to Polichinel. Similar to Havarti, with a deep ivory colour; creamy, supple, buttery texture; and sweet lactic taste, Butter Cheese is a traditional cheese of Germany, often served at breakfast with hearty toast. Beautiful packaging dresses up what would otherwise be a boring small-loaf format. It tells how the cheesemaker created Polichinel years after he discovered it, on the eve of his retirement.

São Miguel

Portuguese Cheese
Toronto, ON

This unique and delightful cheese deserves more attention. Golden in colour, with a savoury, sophisticated burst of sourness that lingers pleasantly, it's so creamy it almost melts in your mouth. São Miguel (pronounced *sow mee-gal*) is made from pasteurized cow milk and is rennet free, using an authentic Portuguese recipe. It is traditionally served as a table cheese and also used for cooking—it's gorgeous melted into mashed potatoes.

Cheese FAQ: What makes a cheese orange?

Annatto is the natural colouring that has been used for centuries to tint cheese curd. It comes from the seed of a tropical plant that is high in carotene. Although annatto is flavourless, it is often hard to convince some people of this.

Tasting Notes

Sein d'Hélène

Fromagerie La Moutonnière
Sainte-Hélène-de-Chester, QC

Blended milk from dairy sheep and Jersey cows that live on farms nestled in the mountains of Sainte-Hélène-de-Chester is used to create this unique semi-firm cheese. Its pointy shape represents the two steep hills of the village, which look like breasts. The cheese name is a clever play on the name of the town: *Sein d'Hélène* translates as "Helen's breasts." Before I knew the story, I thought the cheese was a take on the breast-shaped cow milk cheese of Spain, queso tetilla.

This pressed cheese is as interesting as its shape, with a sandy tan edible natural rind, clean aromas of mutton, a dry yet smooth texture, and herbaceous, mildly acidic flavours that are full and round yet at the same time delicate. Both the shape and the flavours are definite cheeseboard conversation starters!

Fromagerie La Montonière

An original factory recipe, Verdelait combines attributes of Cheddar, Gouda and Raclette to create a versatile table and cooking cheese. Unassuming in flavour, it is a perfect carrier for spices like premium cracked pepper, which provides a slightly warm kick to the cheese. It's a personal favourite of mine to serve with full-bodied Canadian red wines.

Verdelait with Cracked Pepper

Natural Pastures Cheese
Courtenay, BC

Dairy Farmers of Canada

Original Havarti versus Creamy Havarti

Back in the 1970s the Danes added milkfat to traditional Tilsit Havarti to tone down its flavour for the unsophisticated North American palate (it's a similar story to Brie). While I can't disagree with the success of this immensely popular cheese—now available in every flavour under the sun—I just wish that the original version with its slight smear on the exterior was available in Canada (Esrom from Denmark is somewhat similar), especially now that our cheese appreciation levels are on the rise.

Dairy Farmers of Canada

Washed Rind Cheese 4

Dairy Farmers of Canada · MAPAQ

All You Need to Know about Washed Rind Cheese

Washed rind cheeses can be found in the soft, semi-soft and firm families of natural cheese. Their common trait is that they are surface ripened by frequent washing of the cheese with cultured brine, salt brine or another liquid during the curing process to develop the characteristic rind and flavour of the cheese. The bacteria culture in the wash is usually a strain of *Brevibacterium linens* (abbreviated to *B. linens*), which accounts for the pinkish orange colour many of the rinds exhibit. Washed rind cheese in the firm category, such as Alpindon, Five Brothers and 1608, start off being washed to develop their rind and flavour, then at a certain point washing ends and the rind is allowed to dry while the cheese matures.

In October 2012 I was in France auditing a new English-language cheese class offered by the world-renowned company Mons Fromager-Affineur. A prime focus was *l'affinage*, the period of ripening during which cheeses are brushed, scrubbed, washed, turned and re-turned to bring out their best characteristics and flavour. Even though my experience lasted only a couple of weeks, seeing a stage in the metamorphosis of various cheeses every day deepened my respect for the patient art of *affinage*. For one thing, washing cheese isn't like wiping the kitchen counter; it requires great attention to detail, precise motions and the proper amount of brine or wash on the sponge, cloth or brush.

There is no doubt in my mind that Canada, and more specifically Quebec, is on its way to achieving international distinction for washed rind cheese, on a level even greater than our reputation for Cheddar. For centuries France held this honour, led by monks who perfected the process and

then taught it to peasants who were struggling to nourish themselves.

It was also monks who brought the art of washing cheese to Canada, but today the craft is in the capable hands of cheesemakers (some of whom studied the craft in Europe) who practise the time-honoured process to create new, distinctive cheese varieties. While researching this book I asked cheesemongers if there were too many similar Canadian washed rind cheeses. The answer was a resounding "no." The sentiment is that exceptional ones are leading category growth, but competition in this relatively young Canadian cheese category is good, motivating everyone to get better, to master their cheesemaking. As well, there is a consensus among cheesemongers that a locally handcrafted washed rind cheese will always be a draw in its region, even if it is not among the most noteworthy ones.

What's on Your Cheeseboard?

Kelsie Parsons
Cheesemonger, Sobeys
Cheese Blogger,
cheeseandtoast.com, Kitchener

Five Brothers
Old Grizzly
Le Baluchon

It has been said that people outside Quebec do not like washed rind cheese. Indeed, early sales of washed rinds were hurt by retailers who cut and wrapped them like Cheddar (in plastic, with long sell-by or packed-on dates) and displayed them for too long. This was partly because the cheesemakers provided little support in terms of signage, tastings, product knowledge and handling techniques. This has improved, and washed rinds in all degrees of strength and aroma have become the darlings of both novice and experienced caseophiles.

Ripening of semi-soft and firm washed rinds is complex because these cheeses are both surface and interior ripened at the same time (both from the outside rind inwards and from the heart of the cheese outwards). The bacteria cultures, cheesemaking technique and washing frequency may vary among types, but the process is similar: when young cheeses are washed, they are also flipped over so the rind gets the oxygen it needs to develop evenly. As the cheese matures it is washed less often, although flipping and/or wiping or brushing may continue.

While most cheeses are washed with salt water and/or cultured brine, other substances—such as beer, wine and cider—may also be used, with the beverage imparting its special essence to the rind and, eventually, to the cheese paste. The frequency and duration of washing depend on the size and family of the cheese. In every case, crafting these cheeses is a hands-on, labour-intensive work of art.

Untangling the three families of washed rinds can be confusing, but here's a summary (you may also want to refer to Appendix B, "The Significance of Moisture Level," on page 226):

- Soft washed rinds are uncooked, unpressed cheeses that get frequent washes (often daily) for a short period of time (days to a few weeks). Often the rind is rather thin, like a peach or nectarine skin; it will have vegetal notes and is delightfully edible. I have included soft mixed rinds (bloomy/washed combos) with the washed rinds in this chapter. They are often the most aromatic and have the shortest shelf life of washed rinds: a few weeks to three months.
- Semi-soft washed rinds are uncooked, sometimes pressed cheeses that are washed for a longer period of time (weeks to months) but less frequently (every few days rather than daily) than the soft washed rinds. The rind is thicker, still edible but generally more pronounced and rustic in flavour. These cheese are aromatic and their flavour becomes more pronounced as they age: typically four to six months.

- Firm washed rinds start with cheese curd that is sometimes cooked but is always pressed in its cheese mould to allow for a drier curd that can be aged many months. Once removed from the mould, the cheese gets regular washes, like the semi-soft. However, dry brushing or wiping replaces washing at a certain point, to allow the rind to dry and become thicker. The final rind is then considered to be a natural rind, that is, allowed to form on its own, without any special treatments. Edibility of the rind depends on the cheese type; sometimes it's heavenly and sometimes it's too thick or tough—in which case, cut it off and simmer it in stews or soups to add extra flavour.

Heirloom Cheese: The Washed Rind Family

At the 2013 Slow Food Cheese Festival in Bra, Italy, I attended a workshop on UK cheese where two Lancashire cheeses were compared (really, it could have been any two same-name cheeses from any country). The industrial cheese tasted fine and was certainly popular, but the farmstead cheese had a totally awesome depth of flavour! It was then explained that the industrial cheese, and industrial cheese-making in general, depends on heavy use of starter cultures and a fast fermentation method, while farmstead cheese uses a minimum of starter so that the taste of the milk is brought out in slow fermentation. Both styles of cheese serve a purpose in the market, but it is extremely important for consumers to appreciate the difference in styles of the same cheese, so they can understand why there is such a cost difference between industrial and artisan cheese.

The bottom line is that if you want a fine cheese, look to products that are artisan-handcrafted, from an artisan farmstead, or made from raw milk. It is no different from buying wine, beer or bread. Different levels in the quality equation serve specific consumer purposes. To put it another way, you might buy a fifty-dollar or a fifteen-dollar bottle of wine, depending on the occasion. Only if you know the parameters of quality differentiation can you appreciate a finer product.

Heirloom Cheese in This Family

Morbier (France)

Traditionally made from leftover curd of Comté production, this classic washed rind PDO cheese is superior when made from raw cow milk, with a supple, creamy paste and nutty to hay-like to vegetal flavours and aromas. Today the ash line through the centre is decorative, but in the 18th century the ash protected the morning production cheese curd in the moulds from pests and prevented it from forming a top rind. Later the evening leftover Comté curd was placed on top. The popularity of Morbier today allows production on its own account rather than from leftover curd.

Munster (France)

Very different from the semi-firm slicing cheese Muenster, this PDO sticky, aromatically pungent washed rind cheese is Munster (say *muhn-ster* for both). It was first made 800 years ago in the mountains of Alsace by the monks of Munster (the name translates loosely as "monastery" in German), who taught the technique to local villagers. The body starts off firm and supple, becoming creamy with age. In the same league as French Époisses, Munster is loaded with complex, tangy flavours that are sweet, beefy and savoury.

Mutschli (Switzerland)

Nearly every small alpine meadow has its own special cheese, and Mutschli is one of them. These raw cow milk cheeses are known together as Bergkase ("mountain cheese"); they are usually hard, with few holes and washed rinds. They are eaten only in the region of production. How lucky we are that Gunn's Hill Artisan Cheese has brought an excellent version of this elusive cheese to Canada, under the name Handeck!

Reblochon (France)

In the Middle Ages, farmers paid rent or taxes in milk. When the tax collector or landlord came, the farmers would pretend to milk the cows until they were dry in order to pay up. After the collector left, the farmers would re-milk the cows and make a rich, milky cheese from the remaining milk. The cheese

What's on Your Cheeseboard?

Alain Besré
Cheesemonger
Directeur–Marketing Aux Terroirs, Québec and Montréal, QC

**Tomme de Grosse-Île
Grey Owl
1608**

became known as Reblochon, meaning "second milking." This smooth and creamy PDO mountain cheese uses cow milk that is high in fat and protein, from the same breeds as Comté and Beaufort (Montbéliarde, Abondance and Tarentaise), and it is now made from both pasteurized and raw milk. The supple, smooth paste has a somewhat eggy taste, with complex savoury meat or bacon-like saltiness, and is encased in a thin beige washed rind. This cheese excels in June through January.

Taleggio (Italy)

One of Italy's few washed rind cheeses, Taleggio is mentioned in Roman writings from the tenth century CE. It is classified in Italy as a stracchino cheese, meaning that it uses evening cow milk, said to be the richer; "tired" milk of cows that have been in pasture all day. This PDO cheese has

Cheese FAQ: How can I tell when a washed rind cheese is 'over the hill' (beyond *à point*)?

Use your senses when you buy cheese as well as when you eat it. Avoid these sensory attributes:

- **appearance**: grey or irregularly coloured paste; slimy or overly sticky rind; cracked, hard rind; sunken interior (possibly cause by wrapping the cheese in plastic for too long)
- **aroma**: smells of ammonia; overly aggressive or putrid smell that's not characteristic of a cheese
- **feel**: excessive sandiness of the rind; too firm or hard a body (especially by the rind) for the variety of cheese
- **taste**: bitter-tasting rind and/or interior curd; a dominant saltiness

a distinctive square shape with a semi-soft body and bulging sides of orangey rind. The silky texture and sweet egg to buttery saline flavours are more delicate than the aroma; it becomes full-flavoured, with fruity, beefy and pleasantly sour layers of taste, with a few months of age.

Tête de Moine (Switzerland)

Created in 1136, the name (meaning "monk's head") of this cheese came after the French Revolution, from a practice in which farmers paid an annual tax of one cheese per monk in their area for use of the recipe. This firm to hard cheese is made from raw cow milk. Specific temperature and humidity conditions during its three to six months of aging bring out nutty, fruity, tangy and earthy flavours. This PDO cheese is traditionally served using a special circular cutter called a *girolle* to shave the cheese into paper-thin florettes, or petals, in order to maximize its complex flavours. Say *tet duh mwahn*.

Tomme de Savoie (France)

This specific cheese is one of many small or *tomme* cheeses made in the Haute-Savoie region. The milk used is generally what is left over after production of the large wheels of Beaufort. Soft and supple when young, this cheese becomes firmer with age, with layers of milky, nutty, savoury flavours that melt in your mouth. Buying tip: look for labels that say *fabriqué* (made) and *affiné* (aged) in Savoie to ensure the authentic PDO product.

Torta del Casar and Queso de la Serena (Spain)

These stunning PDO raw sheep milk cheeses from Extremadura in western Spain are considered a delicacy even in Spain. The small wheels start off as semi-soft, progressing to soft. The sides will bulge, and when it's really supple, the top rind is cut off like a lid so the thick, luscious paste can be spooned out (which is why buying a full wheel of this cheese is important). Flavours are rich and full, with sour, nutty and floral notes along with hints of mutton and a pleasant bitter finish of cardoon thistle (which the sheep eat as they graze). The thistle magically replaces the need for rennet during cheesemaking. Queso de la Serena is less acid and more buttery than Torta del Casar; to me it's more like Secret de Maurice, made by Maurice Dufour. Say *tort-ah del kah-sar*.

Vacherin Fribourgeois (Switzerland)

Hailing from the canton of Fribourg, this cheese was used 1,000 years ago as the basic food of its time, cheese fondue. This firm, gnarly PDO washed rind cheese must be made from the raw milk of Fribourg cows (a type of Holstein) and washed and turned for three to four months. Unfortunately, this magnificent cheese is on the "endangered species" list of cheeses because it is so difficult to make. Aromas of milk with animal notes, a silky smooth texture, and slightly sour milky flavours that linger as bold but not overpowering make this definitive cheese an experience to remember. Say *vash-ran free-boor-zhwah*.

Handling and Storing Washed Rind Cheese

Like the bloomy rinds in Chapter 2, these cheeses need air to allow the rind to breathe or else they become bitter. Wrapping them in parchment or waxed paper is recommended, as is enjoying them within one week of purchase. Place wrapped pieces in a plastic container to help control the aroma, but remember to keep the air in by not "burping" the container, and be sure the container is about three times larger than the amount of cheese.

To protect against embarrassing "stinky fridge syndrome" from your washed rind cheese, place discarded ends of celery or fennel on a small plate in the fridge (uncovered), or keep a bunch of fresh mint in the cheese drawer, as well as an opened box of baking soda.

If the rind is overly "sandy" it needs moisture (remember, it is used to regular baths). Place a damp paper towel in the storage container, or cover the cheese lightly with a slightly damp tea towel for 30 minutes before serving, to dissolve the salt crystals.

The Perfect Food

Natural cheese, as a concentrated form of milk, is a perfect food, made from the first substance we are fed when we're born. Cheese provides high-quality protein and calcium for healthy bones, and few other foods provide both these nutrients in significant quantities. The only nutrients that cheese lacks are vitamin C and fibre, which are easily added to the diet.

MAPAQ

Populations with the highest longevity (Greeks, Spanish, Italians and French) eat the most cheese, and much less meat than North Americans. Also, the cheeses eaten are made from raw sheep or goat milk, and/or their rinds provide live cultures to enhance digestion.

Readers who are lactose intolerant might be interested to know that lactose (milk sugar) is largely removed with the whey during cheesemaking. The small amount of lactose in the curd is transformed to lactic and other acids by bacterial action during ripening, so semi-soft, firm and hard varieties of cheese contain an insignificant amount of lactose.

Milk products, including cheese, have a role in the prevention of type 2 diabetes. In addition, full-fat dairy products seem to offer protection against weight gain in normal-weight women (Reuters Specialty Food News, January 13, 2007), build intestinal flora, fight dental cavities, reduce the risk of breast and colon cancer, prevent kidney stones and combat gout. Publications such as the New England Journal of Medicine are studying cheese, milk and dairy products to determine their role in disease prevention and everyday nutrition.

Washed Rind Cheese with Canadian Wine and Beer

Soft washed rinds originated in the Alsace region of Europe. A spicy but fruity Gewürztraminer is a classic pairing. Or try aromatic, fruity off-dry white wines such as Riesling or Vidal. Light, earthy reds such as Pinot Noir work with the more earthy, flavourful cheeses, especially if there is a hint of fruit in the wine.

Semi-soft to firm washed rinds are quite friendly to Canadian wine, although the specific varietals depend somewhat on the age of the cheese and the type of milk used. If the cheese is young, try a fruity white or rosé; if mature, go with fruit-forward reds such as Merlot or Baco Noir. The "good marriage" analogy of food partners helping each other out works well here. If the cheese is tired, an acidic, fruity wine may balance it. If the wine is young and green, the fat in the cheese will make it seem less astringent and fuller in flavour.

Icewines, late-harvest wines and hard apple ciders from Quebec are also terrific companions to all washed rind cheese. The sweet yet acidic spirits tame the rustic earthiness of these cheeses.

Beer is a natural with washed rind cheeses. Most lagers and Trappist varieties are complementary. Beers that are malt-forward lend themselves to full-flavoured washed rinds, as their residual sweetness tames the funk of a big cheese. On the other hand, Belgian beers, with their low-hopped fruitiness and yeasty profile, partner well with mild or young washed rinds. Try hoppy beers for cheeses that have grassy, fruity tastes, and porter or bigger beers for fruity, lingering, complex Alpine-style cheeses. It goes without saying that you should try wine- or beer-washed cheeses with not only the beer or wine they were washed with, but others of similar style or point of origin as well.

Ladder of Cheese Appreciation: Washed Rind Cheese

If you like the heirloom cheese on the bottom rung of the ladder, it is likely that you will enjoy the Canadian cheese on the other rungs. It's not that they necessarily taste the same, but they have similar characteristics such as texture and body. The flavours may be more or less similar, depending on the age of the cheese at the time you taste it.

Ladder 1 - Soft

14 Arpents

Empereur

Chevrochon

Secret de Maurice

Magie de Madawaska

French Reblochon

Ladder 2 - Semi-soft

Tomme de Grosse-Île

Tomme à Rudy

Hercule-de-Charlevoix

Mont Jacob

Paradiso

Italian Taleggio

Ladder 3 - Firm

Alfred le Fermier

Chemin Hatley Road

1608

Louis d'Or

Valbert

French Comté

Tasting Notes

14 Arpents

Fromagerie Médard
Saint-Gédéon, QC

As with so many dairy farmers who start a cheese plant, the start of Fromagerie Médard in 2006 fulfilled a lifelong family dream of processing milk from their farm's cows, raised on land that has been in the family for five generations. Médard's cheese is a reflection of the whole pasteurized milk from Brown Swiss cows that graze in the farm meadow in summer and are fed its dry hay during the winter.

This soft farmstead cheese has a sunny orange washed rind, a square shape and a rich ivory paste, which is creamy and full flavoured, with notes of hazelnut that become more pronounced as it ages beyond 30 days. The cheese is named after a road that borders the dairy, *le chemin 14 Arpents* ("14 acres").

1608 de Charlevoix

Laiterie Charlevoix
Baie-St-Paul, QC

The indigenous pedigree cow of Canada is the Canadienne, first bred by colonists here in 1608. In 1900 there were 500,000 of these ruminants, prized for their fine cheesemaking milk. Sadly, in 2007 only 500 were left, in three herds that were relocated to Charlevoix, Quebec. Laiterie Charlevoix is part of a coalition formed to propagate the breed again, led by Philippe Labbé along with his uncles Jean and Dominique Labbé (the head cheesemaker). They have made it their mission to offer these

Canadian Cheese

remaining *vaches Canadiennes* a great environment in which to thrive, rebuild and become the inspiration for creation of great cheese.

There's good reason for this if 1608 is an example of what can be created with the milk. Non-pasteurized Canadienne cow milk and six months aging bring out layered nuances of fruity, meat-like and vegetal flavours. The firm cheese is large for a washed rind (8 kg), with a deep golden curd—the result of pasture grazing and the breed of cow—encased in a sticky orangey exterior. To learn more about the Canadienne cow project and the organization, go to http://www.vachecanadienne.com.

Mario Duchesne

••••••••••••••••••••••••••••••••••••

Simon-Pierre Bolduc has created a masterpiece cheese that he named after his great-grandfather Alfred Bolduc, *le fermier* ("the farmer"). This farmstead washed rind cheese is made from the raw organic milk of the family's pure-bred Holsteins. A firm cheese, it's aged on wooden boards and washed and turned by hand for six to eight months to bring out the woodsy, savoury balance of roasted hazelnut, hay and herbal flavours that can literally tingle on the tongue in the finish. Do eat the rind—it is wonderfully flavourful.

Sometimes people ask, "How do you define *artisan*?" An important portion

Alfred Le Fermier

Fromagerie La Station de Compton
Compton, QC

of the definition is expressed by the Bolduc family's tradition: their mission is to cultivate the soil, to live on it and to hand it down to future generations in even better condition. The brand logo on most cheese from Fromagerie La Station is a silhouette of Alfred Bolduc imprinted on the rind.

Alpindon

Kootenay Alpine Cheese
Creston, BC

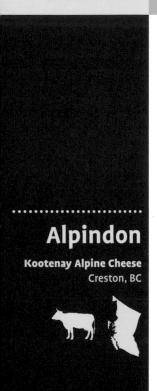

This premium firm organic raw milk cheese is modelled after French Comté and Beaufort d'Alpage. In keeping with centuries of tradition, Alpindon is made using only milk from cows in summer mountain pasture, in a unique cone-shaped cheese vat similar to those used in Europe to make this style of cheese. Alpindon is hand-rubbed and turned during mountain cave aging for a minimum of six months to develop a rich golden interior and a dark textured rind. The texture is smooth, with layers of sweet nut, pasture grass and clover flavour essences. Aging beyond six to twelve months concentrates the flavours, deepens complexity and prompts sweet tyrosine crystal development in the body of the cheese.

Cheesemaking is relatively new at Kootenay (it's been going about seven years), although the Harris family has been farming the land for more than 20 years. The cheesemaking facility was designed so that the milk pipes

use gravity to feed straight from the milk house, saving the carbon impact of transporting milk by truck before it is processed. Solar power provides 70% of the cheese plant's hot water, and heating water accounts for 90% of the plant's energy needs. In addition, the temperature of the aging caves is maintained through geothermal cooling, achieved by circulating well water that is later used for irrigating pasture. These processes make the company environmentally sustainable, on top of its status as organic.

Tasting Notes

Alpine Gold

The Farm House Natural Cheeses
Agassiz, BC

Easy to enjoy and interesting too, this semi-soft washed rind is perfect when you just want something flavourful but comforting in cheese. It has a golden colour on the crust (from the bacteria culture used) and in the paste (from pasteurized Guernsey cow milk), with satisfying earthy flavours. The curd is rinsed during cheesemaking and then the cheese is lovingly brine-washed and turned every other day for six weeks to develop the texture and flavours.

L'Artisan Oka

Agropur
Granby, QC

The lovely balance of the familiar fruity taste of Oka with the sweet, nutty flavour and look of a honeycombed Swiss is achieved in this firm pasteurized cow milk cheese by washing the rind and aging the cheese in the original cellars of the Cistercian abbey in Oka, Quebec. It's best enjoyed at room temperature for full flavour.

Baluchon

Fromagerie F.X. Pichet
Sainte-Anne-de-la-Pérade, QC

This unique farmstead cheese has a golden washed rind and pale yellow interior. The distinctive meaty aroma and multiple layers of lingering vegetal flavour are partly the result of the organic non-pasteurized milk from the family's herd of Brown Swiss and purebred Holstein cows. This is one artisan cheese that is consistent in all aspects, time after time. It was the veg-etal aromatics and flavour of Baluchon (pronounced *bal-oo-shon*) that started my infatuation with vegetables and cheese. To my mind, steamed Brussels sprouts or Savoy cabbage (just warm, not hot) is the perfect companion for this cheese.

Beer Washed Rind Cheeses

The popularity of local beer and cheese has led several cheesemakers to wash some of their semi-soft cheeses with beer from a local brewery. Try them together (ideally with the beer they were washed with) to compare the effects of the different beers on the cheese. Both beer and cheese are living fermented substances that react negatively to plastic wrap. Although I love beer and washed rind cheese, I have found that beer washed cheeses go wonderfully with a crisp white wine such as an off-dry Riesling.

Beau's Beer Washed
An appetizing marriage of Gunn's Hill Oxford's Harvest cheese washed every other day for several weeks with a sea-sonal beer from Beau's All Natural Brew-ing, Vankleek Hill, ON. Essentially this creates a different cheese every season!

Beau's Beer Washed
Gunn's Hill Artisan Cheese
Woodstock, ON

Le Bocké
Fromagerie Champêtre
Le Gardeur, QC

Le Bocké

Hand washed several times with Bock de Joliette amber beer from L'Alchimiste microbrewery for 30 to 40 days. Delicate flavours of roast hazelnut and wild mushroom complement the yeasty aroma of beer in this appealing cheese.

Fêtard
Fromagerie du
Champ à la Meule
Notre-Dames-de-Lourdes, QC

Fêtard

A *fêtard* (pronounced *feh-tar*) is a person of high spirits or a merrymaker, and so is this thermalized milk cheese, which is soaked and washed with Maudite, a strong (8%) Quebec beer from Unibroue. The flavours of this creamy cheese range from melted butter and lactic to tangy, with hints of yeasty bitterness on the finish (from the beer), and become more prominent as the cheese matures.

Brigitte

Best Baa Dairy
Fergus, ON

Made from raw sheep milk and aged 60 days, this luxurious beauty has a pale terracotta washed rind that is damp to the touch, with layers of abundant lingering taste that include straw, mutton and truffle. The texture is dense, with a velvety cream finish. It's a most engaging cheese for anyone who enjoys French Reblochon. And of note is that Best Baa makes each batch of cheese with the sheep milk of one producer. This creates traceability and accountability for each of the co-op farmer members.

The cheese is named for Brigitte, the French cheesemaker who shared numerous techniques with Elisabeth Bzikot, the cheesemaker at Best Baa. Such sharing of knowledge is generous, and common among Old World cheesemakers as they try to keep the traditional art of cheesemaking alive in a modern world full of shortcuts and hurry.

• •

There are 38 new cheeses in this edition of *Canadian Cheese: A Guide*, and Canotier is right near the top of my favourite new finds for its originality—a Cheddar-like consistency in a firm washed rind. This *fromagerie* is known for fine craftsmanship, and they have reproduced an ancestral recipe from the first cheesemakers who arrived on the island early in the 20th century.

As with the other cheese made at Île-aux-Grues, thermalized milk from the island's cows adds a special distinction to the cheese. Aged for one year to bring out the enticing aroma of cultured crème, it has rounded flavours of sweet grass and roast nuts, fruity sweetness and damp wood, which just keep coming and coming across the palate.

The label is a painting by the artist Robert Gagné from Isle-aux-Grues. It shows the transport of materials and mail by ice canoe, the only way to reach the island in winter in the early 1900s.

Canotier de L'Isle

Fromagerie Île-aux-Grues
Isle-aux-Grues, QC

Tasting Notes

Chemin Hatley Road

Fromagerie La Station de Compton
Compton, QC

Another perfect cheese that expresses the magic that small nuances can make in a cheese that sounds like so many others: firm washed rind from thermized organic cow milk. Yet this creation is different, be it because of the bacteria cultures used or the cheesemaker's technique. Yes, it expresses nuts and butter in the aroma, but the balance of savoury floral and sweet fruity flavours, with just the right finish of salt, is unique—even though the descriptive words may sound similar! Hatley Road (a.k.a. *chemin*) was used by stagecoaches travelling between Quebec City and Boston in the early 1900s, and it's also where the farm and cheese factory are located.

Clandestin

Fromagerie Le Détour
Notre-Dame-du-Lac, QC

This velvety textured handcrafted masterpiece is made from a blend of pasteurized cow and rich sheep milk. Barnyard and sheep aromas introduce grassy flavours of straw and butter that melt in the mouth, with just a touch of salt. The thin rind acts like a soft pastry crust around the cheese, integrating paste and rind. Take your time—this cheese is a five-star cheese experience and a Canadian *fromage* that more than answers my frequent cravings for French Reblochon.

Comtomme

Fromagerie La Station de Compton
Compton, QC

This savoury semi-soft washed rind cheese is made with the organic thermized milk of 50 purebred Holstein cows. The herd has been a "closed" herd for more than 40 years. In other words, no new cows have been added since then. As a result, the milk has very specific characteristics that are imparted to the cheese.

Aged three to five months, a coppery-coloured rind surrounds the rich ivory paste. The enticing grassy aroma and the complexity of the milky, fruity and roasted nut flavours signify that fresh milk from the Bolduc dairy farm has been used. Consistent quality over the years makes this cheese a favourite of many.

Tasting Notes

Curé Labelle

Fromagerie Le P'tit Train du Nord
Mont-Laurier, QC

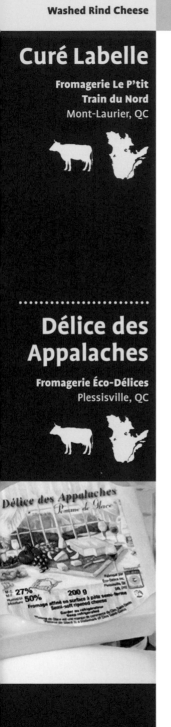

This most unique pasteurized cow milk cheese is named after Bishop Labelle, who was responsible for bringing the railroad into the region and consequently opening it up for trade with Montreal. This semi-soft washed rind (pronounced *kiur-ray la-bell*) is cured over 90 days to bring out distinct layers of flavour from floral and nutlike to meaty, with an aromatic musty mineral aroma. Sadly, it is available only in Quebec.

Délice des Appalaches

Fromagerie Éco-Délices
Plessisville, QC

This artisan delicacy (pronounced *day-leece dez appel-ahsh*) achieves its lingering ripe apple flavour and creamy semi-soft body through daily turning and hand washing with the Quebec apple ice cider, Pomme de Glace, for four to six weeks while being matured on pine boards. Fromagerie Éco-Délices was a local initiative well before the word *locavore* became trendy. The cows producing the milk live on a farm across the road from the cheese factory. The plant equipment was designed by the cheesemaker (in a square configuration for efficiency) and the pictures on the cheese labels are designed by a local artist.

D'Iberville

Au Gré des Champs
Saint-Jean-sur-Richelieu, QC

This farmstead cheese, made with the rich organic raw milk from Brown Swiss cows, is aged for more than 60 days. Brown Swiss is a pedigree cow, like Ayrshire, Guernsey, Jersey and Canadienne, whose milk has the higher fat, protein and other components that cheesemakers value for making premium artisan cheese. D'Iberville has a fruity aroma with flavours that hint of fresh herbs in spring and wildflowers in summer and fall. Daniel Gosselin runs this farm and makes the cheese with Suzanne Dufresne and their daughters, Marie-Pier and Virginie.

Douanier

Fromagerie Fritz Kaiser
Noyan, QC

Fritz Kaiser grew up in Switzerland and moved at a young age to Quebec, where he began making cheese in 1981. This distinctive cheese has an edible washed rind and a thin decorative edible vegetable ash streak through the middle (sadly mistaken by some to be blue mould). Douanier (pronounced *doo-on-nee-yay*) means "customs officer," and is so named because of the plant's proximity to the US border. The smooth texture leads to mellow flavours of roast hazelnut and ripe apple that become more pronounced with age.

Empereur

Fromagerie Fritz Kaiser
Noyan, QC

Kaiser is German for "emperor" and is also the cheesemaker's name. This small disk of cheese (pronounced *om-purr-er*) more than measures up to its royal name, with an aroma of turnip from the tender washed rind contributing to balanced flavours of grass and roasted hazelnut with a hint of salt. Over the years several people have compared it to the Alsace-Lorraine washed rind classic Munster.

Cheese FAQ: What is "light" cheese?

Any cheese with one-third less milkfat than its full-fat counterpart can be considered "light." Lower milkfat in cheese generally reduces flavour and toughens its texture. However, a remarkable **Empereur Light**, with 15% milkfat is made by Fromagerie Fritz Kaiser. At tastings many people have gratefully said, "If you hadn't told me this cheese was lower-fat I wouldn't have guessed it." Another notable reduced-fat cheese is **Zurigo** (page 131), also made by Kaiser.

Ewenity

Best Baa Dairy
Fergus, ON

A change in the finishing process created an entirely new cheese for Best Baa. Ewenity (pronounced *unity*) is the sheep milk Gouda called Eweda (page 165) washed with brine rather than soaked in brine and waxed, as Eweda would be. It is then brushed during ripening, creating a natural rind and a very delightful creamy semi-soft cheese with small pinholes and cream and lactic flavours.

• •

Fleur des Monts

Fromagerie La Moutonnière
Ste-Hélène-de-Chester, QC

This distinctive semi-soft sheep milk gem has a washed rind and is inspired by cheese from the French Pyrenees. It's smooth in texture, with delicate almond and rich sheep milk tastes that seem to comfort as they linger on and on. The flavour develops fine character during curing of three to six months.

• •

Fleur-en-Lait

Glengarry Fine Cheese
Lancaster, ON

To sell milk to Glengarry, you have to be a family farm. The plant uses only fresh milk with high cream and protein content from small farms in the region. The result of this standard can be witnessed in their cheese. This superior orangey-coloured washed rind cheese (pronounced *flurr on lay*), made from pasteurized cow milk, is related to the French cheese St-Paulin. It has a rich yellow interior, buttery texture and rustic aroma, with tempting bitter nut and savoury flavours that offer complexity and linger nicely.

Tasting Notes

Fou du Roy

**Les Fromagiers
de la Table Ronde**
Sainte-Sophie, QC

Pasteurized organic cow milk from the Alary family farm is used to produce this supple rosy-hued washed rind wheel of cheese. Classic aromas of hay and fermented fruit introduce a silky, springy paste with an expressive earthy and nutty flavour. During the aging process, its pink-orange rind is covered with a thin down of whitish grey *Penicillium*. Soft, melt-in-your-mouth cheese paste offers a delightful taste of butter, peanuts and hay, with a slight hint of the barnyard. Pronounce *foo dew rwah*.

Frère Chasseur

Au Gré des Champs
Saint-Jean-sur-Richelieu, QC

This firm Swiss Tête de Moine–style cheese is meant to be served in lacy florets created on a special cheese cutter called a *girolle*. Organic raw cow milk, with natural flora enhanced by six months of aging, makes Frère Chasseur a full-flavoured cheese (like the original) with layers of roasted nut and dried fruit giving way to delicious earthy, barny flavours. It could be denser or harder for easier floret-making, but comparison is hardly fair. The Swiss original has been made for more than 900 years, while Frère Chasseur is less than five years old and is the first North American version of Tête de Moine. Greens such as arugula complement the flavour, while florets dress up a salad plate. If you don't have a *girolle*, use a cheese planer to serve the cheese in paper-thin "petals" to show off the magnificent flavour.

Canadian Cheese

Grand Manitou

Fromagerie La Suisse Normande
Saint-Roch-de-l'Achigan, QC

Inspired by Swiss and French heritage, Suisse Normande makes different types of cheese from cow, goat and sheep milk, which is fairly rare for a single factory. Grand Manitou is a blend of all three milks, creating an unctuous, soft mixed-rind tomme (the generic name for a small wheel of cheese). Flavours are of fresh churned butter and cream, with a bright goat milk tang finale. It's made only in summer, when the animals are grazing in the pasture. To my taste, it is ecstasy in cheese—when you can get it. In the off-season, try Clandestin or Magie du Madawaska.

Gré des Champs

Au Gré Des Champs
Saint-Jean-sur-Richelieu, QC

This cheese is lovingly handcrafted from organic raw milk. Cheesemaker Daniel Gosselin feeds his herd of Brown Swiss cows a special mixture of hay and wild herbs to give the milk (and thus the cheese) a unique sweet, herbal flavour. The beautiful ochre-coloured mixed rind on this firm cheese helps to give the cheese (pronounced *gray day shom*) a subtle lingering hazelnut quality that is delightful, after a mere three months of aging. Unfortunately, the cheese plant is a bit too close to the cow barn and cannot be federally licensed. What a shame to limit availability of the distinguished cheese made by Au Gré des Champs!

Dairy Farmers of Canada

Tasting Notes

Guillaume Tell

Fromagerie Domaine Féodal
Berthierville, QC

Guillaume Tell (pronounced *gee-owm tell*—William Tell in English) is soaked and washed with a fruity Quebec ice cider from the Leduc-Piedimonte domain, which imparts a golden hue under the speckled white bloomy rind. This lovely pasteurized cow milk cheese has a fragrant aroma and flavours of fermented apple, mushroom and cream. It's the perfect Quebec duet.

Harvest Moon

Poplar Grove
Penticton, BC

This boutique cheese plant is nestled in the Poplar Grove Vineyard, on the Naramata Bench in the beautiful Okanagan Valley. Made from pasteurized cow milk, Harvest Moon is a soft, complex washed rind cheese with an earthy aroma. It is washed once a week with brine for three weeks and smeared with cultured brine for another two. The cheese was first made during a full moon and is just like an unforgettable huge moon. It has robust, lingering flavours of wet grass and green cabbage with a finish of salt—remarkably well balanced for a cheese having this much flavour.

Hercule de Charlevoix

Laiterie Charlevoix
Baie-Saint-Paul, QC

Don't let bold aromatics intimidate you from trying Hercule (pronounced *air-kewl duh sharl-uh-vwah*), as the flavour is quite refined. Thermized Jersey milk from the Stessi farm is used to create this firm brine washed rind cheese that is a cross between the classic mountain cheeses Comté and Gruyère. At six months Hercule is somewhat supple, with a fruity aroma and a sweet to tangy finish. At 18 months the body is creamier and more complex, with a full, nutty flavour and an earthy toasted rind that is quite edible if you're into rinds. It's named after the "strong man of Charlevoix," who was a local hero in the late 1700s.

Kenogami

Fromagerie Lehmann
Hébertville, QC

The Lehmann family moved from Switzerland to Lac-St-Jean in 1983. Today the entire family works together to run the farm, from taking care of the animals to producing the milk and making and marketing the cheese. Named after the road that borders Fromagerie Lehmann and pronounced *ken-OH-gam-ee*, this soft surface ripened farmstead cheese is made from the unpasteurized milk of Brown Swiss cows. The rind is orange and the aroma is of aromatic herbs, with a creamy texture and a buttery, nutty flavour. Unfortunately it is available only in Quebec because of provincial licensing and small production capacity. Jacob Lehmann believes that artisan products are a philosophy, a way of life.

Canadian Cheese

Tasting Notes

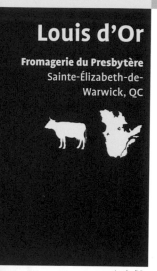

Louis d'Or

Fromagerie du Presbytère
Sainte-Élizabeth-de-
Warwick, QC

Jean-Morin and his brother Dominique are fourth-generation dairy farmers on La Ferme Louis d'Or, named by their grandfather. They have been farming organically for more than 20 years. The decision to make cheese came in 2005 as a way to expand the family business, and the old church rectory of Sainte-Élizabeth-de-Warwick, located directly across from the farm, was the best place to do this. The building was completely remodelled to regain the

Louis d'Or

character it had when it was built in 1936, as well as to meet government standards. The rest is history! Fromagerie du Presbytère began making history with their prize-winning cheese, while never losing sight of the community that supports them through their popular Friday night cheese and wine socials, celebrating life, friendship and cheese!

Organic raw cow milk from the Louis d'Or family farm is the start of what makes this firm farmstead cheese exceptional. It comes in an impressive 40-kilogram wheel format (like classic Comté from Jura, France) with the name Louis d'Or elegantly engraved into the orange-tan rind. The full aroma and taste at nine months of age is reminiscent of newly mown grass, sweet milk and rich nuts that last on the palate. Typical of a well made cheese, the flavours ramp up exquisitely, with caramel on the finish, by the maximum age of two years. The rind is edible (vegetal, tasting of celery and earth) and should be enjoyed. This remarkable cheese is also available in a fondue format made with organic beer and cleverly packaged in a black church-shaped box, ready to simply heat, stir and enjoy!

Tasting Notes

Magie de Madawaska

Fromagerie Le Détour
Notre-Dame-du-Lac, QC

Jersey cow milk gives this thin disk of cheese a velvety texture. Magie de Madawaska (pronounced *ma-zhee duh ma-da-wha-ska*) is handcrafted to deliver rich, grassy to slightly earthy flavours inside the washed rind. *Madawaska* means "country of lakes and rivers," and it's another five-star cheese experience from Fromagerie Le Détour. Depending on the season, sweet wild-flowers or savoury herbal back-notes dominate the flavour. Try this cheese monthly from June through November, and take note of the changes to witness how what an animal eats is reflected in the cheesemilk and also the cheese.

Mamirolle

Fromagerie Éco-Délices
Plessisville, QC

The unique process used to create Mamirolle was developed in France in 1935. Éco-Délices has produced this cheese since 1996 and holds the only Canadian licence to do so. The creamy texture, supple body and earthy aromatics of this cheese (pronounced *mam-ear-rol*) develop with hand washing, turning and aging on pine boards for three to four weeks. The flavour is mild and fruity when young and rich, grassy and very aromatic when aged for 80 to 90 days.

This unique handmade thermized cow milk soft cheese has dual rinds—bloomy and washed. Its complex, slightly bitter flavours of mushroom and deep roast hazelnut are complemented by the salty sea-spray influences of local grasses the cows (who live on the Île-aux-Grues islands) ingest. Mi-Carême (pronounced *mee carr-em*) is a traditional Acadian holiday similar to Mardi Gras; French settlers originally brought it to Quebec and it is still celebrated on Isle-aux-Grues.

· ·

Crafted from the milk of cows pastured in the Charlevoix region, this consistently perfect semi-soft cheese (pronounced *mee-nya-ron duh sharl-e-vwah*) has a straw-coloured washed rind and dense ivory interior. Cured a minimum of 50 days, its delicate aroma is of cream and yogurt, giving way to subtle buttery, nutty flavours with gentle fruity undertones. The excellence of Migneron, created in 1995, helped pave the way for public appreciation of the washed rind cheese family outside Quebec, which is a significant achievement. *Merci beaucoup*, Maurice!

Mi-Carême

Fromagerie Île-aux-Grues
Isle-aux-Grues, QC

· · · · · · · · · · · · · · · · · · · ·

Migneron de Charlevoix

Maison d'Affinage
Maurice Dufour
Baie-St-Paul, QC

Miranda

Fromagerie Fritz Kaiser
Noyan, QC

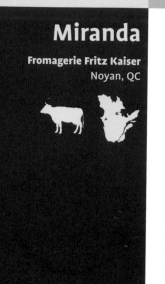

The signature cheese in Fritz's cellar, this amazing pasteurized cow milk cheese has a rust-coloured rind covering the firm, dense ivory paste. The flavours are richly nutty to pleasantly fruity, developed slowly by washing every few days during the 8 to 12 month curing period. In the 1600s the town of Noyan was part of the region of Miranda, hence the cheese's name. A noble comparison to this cheese might be that outstanding classic of Switzerland Vacherin Fribourgeois.

Mont-Jacob

Fromagerie Blackburn
Jonquière, QC

Named for the mountain across from the factory and made with pasteurized cow milk, this semi-firm washed rind cheese has a dense body, smooth texture, delicate aroma and complex, lingering buttery sweetness. It becomes more supple and tangy as it ages, developing roasted hazelnut and dry fruit flavours. Mont-Jacob (pronounced *mone-jah-kob*) is a beautiful cheese that is easily damaged by being wrapped in plastic.

The name (pronounced *moo-tone roozh*) is a fun wordplay on the name of the famous nightclub in Paris—*mouton* is French for "sheep" and *rouge* means "red," like the rusty red rind of the cheese. It's a firm raw sheep milk cheese with a lightly yellow creamy paste that ripens from inside the wheel outwards to the rind (interior ripened). Somewhat stinky (in the good, washed rind sense), there's an aroma of wet grass, with complex layers of flavour from meaty to nutty and grassy with a sea-salt finish—titillating and memorable on the tongue!

Mouton Rouge

Best Baa Dairy
Fergus, ON

Niagara Gold

Upper Canada Cheese
Jordon Station, ON

With this cheese, handcrafted from the milk of Guernsey cows, it's the milk that is largely responsible for its singular flavour. Guernseys are renowned for producing ultra-rich milk for cheesemaking. The milk is also influenced by the local terroir of the Niagara Escarpment (mineral limestone), ingested by the cows through the pasture grasses they enjoy. The wheels of cheese are hand washed and turned regularly during four months of ripening to create the aromatic golden washed rind and complex sweet, grassy to fruity flavours that become more pronounced with age.

Tasting Notes

Noyan

Fromagerie Fritz Kaiser
Noyan, QC

MAPAQ

It's easy to overlook gentle giants like Noyan among more assertive members of the washed rind group. Named after the town in Quebec where it's made, this beautiful sand-coloured washed rind with pink hues has small pinholes in the ivory body. It delivers a rich, pleasing taste of cultured milk, mushroom and sweet roasted nuts, which becomes more assertive as the cheese matures. This cheese is a real crowd-pleaser.

Oka Classique

Agropur
Granby, QC

First made by Cistercian Trappist monks in 19th-century Quebec, this semi-soft washed rind cheese is one of Canada's most famous. It has a slightly bolder flavour than regular Oka because of its extra washing and aging (more than 60 days). Classique has a creamy texture and flavours of butter, nuts and apple that become more pronounced with age. Sometimes the rind on this cheese has a slightly gritty or sandy texture in the mouth. Not to worry, it's just the rind needing moisture after weeks of regular baths. Remedy it, if you want, with a light wipe from a slightly damp paper towel.

Canadian Cheese

This handcrafted pasteurized cow milk washed rind cheese is modelled after a little-known cheese from Switzerland called Mutschli. Mild and creamy, the lightly lactic, buttery and dried apple flavour notes develop after only six weeks of aging on cedar wood planks. A nice starter washed rind cheese with low aromatics for the uninitiated caseophile.

Oxford's Harvest

Gunn's Hill Artisan Cheese
Woodstock, ON

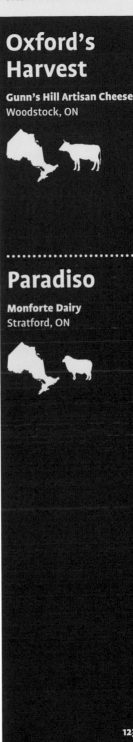

This semi-soft sheep milk creation is a variation on the Italian classic cheese Taleggio. Its distinctive square shape has a washed rind speckled with blue and pink moulds. Handmade in Ontario, the cheese has a musty aroma and buttery texture that lead to a complex array of lingering herbal to meaty and lactic, tart flavours. This cheese really likes to breathe; rewrap it in waxed or parchment paper, then put in a large self-sealing bag or plastic container with some air left inside.

Paradiso

Monforte Dairy
Stratford, ON

Tasting Notes

Peau Rouge

Les Dépendances
St-Hubert, QC

The collaboration of cheesemaker and *affineur* practised in Europe for centuries comes to life in this fantastic semi-firm washed rind cheese. Jean-Philippe Gosselin of Les Dépendances has a young cheese made to his specifications by master cheesemaker Fritz Kaiser from pasteurized cow milk. After it has matured for three months at the Kaiser facility, Mr. Gosselin takes the best wheels to his facility, where he finishes the cheese—the practice called *affinage*—in his caves for 10 to 12 months, washing, turning and brushing the rind in ideal airflow, temperature and humidity conditions. The result of this partnership is a rich roasted hazelnut to fruity cheese (pronounced *poe roozgeh*) with grassy notes and a lovely sprinkling of crystals in the body.

Pied-de-Vent

Fromagerie du Pied-de-Vent
Havre-aux-Maisons, QC

In the Magdalen Islands the expression *pied de vent* refers to the sun's rays piercing through the clouds. This soft washed rind cheese is made from the fresh milk of a single herd of Canadienne cows fed a diversity of fodder from the Magdalen Islands. More interesting in the summer, when the cows are in pasture, Pied-de-Vent (pronounced *pee-ah-duh-vahn*) is a distinctive cheese that reflects the unique terroir of the islands, with an earthy aroma and a delightfully lingering flavour of floral grasses and wet hay. The rind does get bitter easily, so enjoy the cheese as soon as you buy it, and definitely avoid wrapping it in plastic.

Soft and distinctive with its square shape, thick, supple body and mixed rind, this aromatic farmstead cheese (pronounced *wrong dez eel*) is made from whole pasteurized Brown Swiss cow milk. Mild yet complex, its dry hay, butter and earthy mushroom flavours fill the mouth with lingering pleasure.

Located on Vancouver Island, Little Qualicum's cheese is available only in British Columbia. The facility has made a wide range of cheeses since 2001, shortly after Clarke and Nancy Gourlay returned from living in Switzerland. This farmstead company milks a small mixed herd of Holstein, Ayrshire, Brown Swiss and Canadienne cows, makes cheese and operates Morningstar Farm, a family park with self-guided tours, festivals and events, lots of farm animals to see and pet, a beautiful picnic area and a trail for strolling around the 68 acres.

Inspired by Swiss Gruyère—it has a predominant sweet nut taste—with distinct Cheddar traits (a dense, firm

Rang des Îles

Fromagerie Médard
Saint-Gédéon, QC

Rathtrevor

Little Qualicum Cheeseworks
Parksville, BC

body). Rathrevor is a pleasingly novel washed rind cheese made from raw cow milk and aged six months. Golden in colour, the texture is smooth, with tangy, herbaceous flavours and a hint of garlic on the finish.

Secret de Maurice

Maison d'Affinage Maurice Dufour
Baie-St-Paul, QC

The secret of this unctuous 100% pasteurized sheep milk cheese comes from the mountains of western Spain where Maurice Dufour travelled to learn the art of making a fairly obscure, soft sheep milk cheese called Torta del Casar, which has long been in my top ten of favourite European cheeses, along with its cousin Queso de la Serena.

While the flavour and texture of this cheese are remarkable enough—delicate cultured butter and nut tastes delivered in silky pudding-like ribbons of cheese—the unusual way you eat this "torta-style" cheese is certain to make it memorable: gently cut through the top of the rind, then peel away the "lid" and scoop out the luscious cheese with a spoon onto hearty bread or broccoli florets. The empty rind is very edible, with delicious hay and fruit notes. It is often fought over when I serve the cheese.

This raw Jersey cow milk cheese is a washed rind stinker (in a good, cheesy, barnyard way), but as usual, the flavour is milder than the aroma. Traditional production methods include the use of rennet, not microbial enzyme. The mottled tan and white rustic crust hides a rich yellow paste with long, full layers of flavours: cultured cream and meat stock and roasted nuts. This gem satisfies the desire for a full-flavoured washed rind with power and no lingering off flavour, just more of the same lovely balance.

The distinctive one-of-a-kind flavour of this farmstead cheese is due to the thermalized milk of Brown Swiss cows from the Lilogru farm, which are fed exclusively on the salty hay (*foin de batture*) from the island's shore. The ivory-coloured creamy paste is encased in an edible tan brushed mixed rind, presenting a musty damp grass aroma and flavours that are slightly acidic and fruity, mixed with notes of earthy mushroom that unfold with leisure on the palate. The name was chosen to commemorate the thousands of Irish immigrants buried on Grosse-Île. If there were a PDO system for Canadian cheese, Tomme de Grosse-Île would qualify; the unique flavour of this cheese can be produced only with milk

Tomme à Rudy

Ferme Ducrêt
Saint-Basile-de-Portneuf, QC

Tomme de Grosse-Île

Fromagerie Île-aux-Grues
Isle-aux-Grues, QC

from cows fed *foin de batture*, and the cheesemaker has delivered consistent, incredible-tasting cheese since the late 1990s. The touching true story of this cheesemaker can be found in Margaret Webb's book *Apples to Oysters: A Food Lover's Tour of Canadian Farms*.

Valbert

Fromagerie Lehmann
Hébertville, QC

This firm cheese from thermized Brown Swiss cow milk is very reminiscent of a 10-to-12-month Comté, even when aged only six months! It's encased in a rust-coloured washed—and totally glorious to eat—rind with the name Valbert embossed around the perimeter. It has melt-in-your-mouth earthy (possibly a special *B. linens* culture), fruity and nutty flavours, with a few granules in the dense golden body. Comté has been made since the ninth century, and Valbert less than two decades! Such a marvellous achievement in a cheese relies on a balance of the plants (the land), the animals and the humans who care enough to bring it all together.

• •

My associate and Cheese Education Guild graduate Debbie Levy introduced Victor to me by saying that it is *the* cheese, over all others, that she and her husband savour on special occasions, usually with tawny port, because of the fond memories it brings back. This is so true. Many people say that cheese connects them to places they have been, good times they have enjoyed, or special people they have met. Emotional memory is a documented factor in cheese appreciation.

Martin Guilbault, a pioneer in Quebec artisan cheesemaking, handcrafts this exquisite thermalized cow milk cheese. The name Victor et Berthold is a tribute to the generations of Guilbaults who once ran the family farm: Victor, grandfather of *fromagerie* founder Martin Guilbault, and Berthold, his uncle. The semi-soft body within the washed rind is rich and smooth. The aroma is of butter, while the taste starts off as subtly herbal to grassy, developing rich earthy, barnlike notes as the cheese matures beyond its 60-day minimum age. The rind is edible and enhances the flavour of the cheese, although it suffers if bought or stored in plastic wrap.

• •

Victor et Berthold

Fromagerie du Champ à la Meule
Notre-Dames-de-Lourdes, QC

Tasting Notes

Wine Washed 1812

Gunn's Hill Artisan Cheese
Woodstock, ON

Imagine Gunn's Hill Oxford's Harvest (page 123), washed right after cheese-making for several weeks with Palatine Hills Chardonnay from Niagara to develop the pleasant fruity taste in this pasteurized cow milk cheese. Try Oxford and 1812 side by side—perhaps with the Beau's Beer Washed version (page 103) as well—to check out the difference a wash can make in the same cheese.

Zacharie Cloutier

Fromagerie Nouvelle France
Racine, QC

Marie-Chantal and Jean-Paul Houde are a brother and sister team in their twenties whose family background is steeped in agriculture. Jean-Paul started the *bergerie* (sheep farm) and Marie-Chantal the *fromagerie* (cheese factory). Zacherie Cloutier is their first cheese (named after a family ancestor), and it's plain to see they are off to a great start!

Some cheesemongers say it is like Manchego, which is also made with sheep milk; both have a dense, firm body and zigzag-patterned rind. Manchego is one of my cheese staples, and I think the resemblance stops there because Zacharie has its own exciting personality. It's creamier and less dry, with buttery, sweet nut notes and underlying hints of wood and caramel after six months aging. Perhaps it's the use of thermalized East Friesian sheep milk that allows the local terroir to

Canadian Cheese

shine through. (Sadly, most of the Manchego available now, though still made from Manchega sheep milk, is pasteurized and of industrial quality.) Zacharie has an orangey washed rind that credits the cheesemaker for having done some "custom finishing." Eating the rind on Zacharie is optional; it's often pleasant but sometimes picks up off flavours.

••••••••••••••••••••••••••••••••••••••

Another great alternative in a 15% fat-reduced cheese, this semi-soft washed rind cheese has a supple, smooth texture—especially compared to the rubbery texture of some semi-soft fat-reduced cheeses—a milky aroma and balanced flavours of hay and salted butter.

••••••••••••••••••••••

Zurigo

Fromagerie Fritz Kaiser
Noyan, QC

More Fun Than S'mores

The Swiss are the most interactive caseophiles on earth, with a uniquely wide variety of cheese meal traditions such as fondue, Tête de Moine shaved into pretty lacy curls (using a girolle, a special circular cutter), and Raclette, which is both a semi-soft washed rind cheese and a way to serve it. At a Raclette party everyone cooks their own meal on a special grill that melts the cheese, which is then drizzled over boiled potatoes. Some Raclette grills also have a griddle for sautéing vegetables such as zucchini or mushrooms. It's a very convivial way to entertain, with minimal preparation required. Some cheesemongers will rent you a Raclette grill when you buy the cheese.

Raclette can be enjoyed as a table cheese, but the buttery, hazelnut-to-fruity goodness of this washed rind cheese comes alive when it is heated. In Canada we have several fine Raclette cheeses. I recommend Fritz Kaiser's Raclette Griffon (washed in Griffon beer); Fromagerie La Station's Raclette de Compton, made from thermized organic milk in Natural or Au Poivre (black pepper); or Little Qualicum Raclette—they all resist "oiling off" when heated.

Keeping It Simple

Fromagerie F.X. Pichet, Fromagerie Île-aux-Grues, Fromagerie La Station Compton, Fromagerie Éco-Délices and La Maison Maurice Dufour are all excellent examples of cheesemakers with discipline. They offer one, two or three cheeses, delivering consistent quality and flavour each and every time. Bravo! This trait is not popular in the Canadian artisan cheesemaking world. But if cheese history has taught us anything, mastery is the key to quality and profitability. The great cheesemakers of Europe make one style and often only one type of cheese. Regional and individual excellence arises from this—think Roquefort, Gruyère, Manchego, Comté, Camembert and so on.

In my experience, novice cheesemakers (roughly anyone with less than five years' experience) typically focus on too many cheeses before fully understanding their milk, their plant, the specifics of cheesemaking and ripening for their cheese, and the cheese that is best suited to their milk and terroir. The wine industry used to have this same problem, but now boutique wineries are finding their points of excellence.

Oka or Trappist?

The same cheese by a different name—or is it? Oka was once, along with Cheddar, the Canadian cheese industry's claim to fame. This indigenous washed rind had a taste that was full and earthy, with a distinct fruitiness. Then, in 1981, the rights to the cheese, as well as the monastery where it was made, were bought by the Quebec dairy farmer co-operative Agropur. The original cheese "went missing," according to its many devoted fans, until a loyal customer from Toronto, Yves Étienne Massicotte, who happened to be a film producer, hunted it down at Notre-Dame des Prairies monastery in Manitoba. He made a documentary about the cheese called *A Monk's Secret*, thus preserving this original slice of Canadian cheese history. The amazing original raw-milk Oka (now called Trappist) is now available only in Manitoba.

Dairy Farmers of Canada

Agropur

Firm
Cheese 5

Dairy Farmers of Canada

All You Need to Know about Canadian Firm Cheese

Substantial, honest and dependable—like Canadians, eh? Any discussion of Canadian firm cheese has to start with Cheddar, but really the family is huge, dominated by popular cow milk cheeses such as provolone, Gouda and Swiss, along with emerging classics from the goat and sheep quadrants.

There are many different properties to firm cheese, but all have approximately the same moisture content (35 to 52%) and milkfat level (an exception is fat-reduced cheese, page 131). Each type employs a specific method for whey removal beyond the use of enzymes, such as aggressive curd cutting and/or milling, cooking the curd at a high temperature during cheesemaking, or applying heavy pressure to the cheese in its mould to force out all the whey and create the dense body.

Bacteria cultures, the particular cheesemaking technique and the ripening process are specific to an individual style of cheese. Firm cheeses have a solid, dense body (with the exception of Swiss cheese styles and sometimes Gouda), are usually large—most Canadian Cheddar is made in 290-kilogram blocks and Swiss in 40-kilogram blocks or wheels—and made frequently from raw or thermized milk, because they can easily be aged for more than 60 days.

Historically, while fresh or unripened cheeses used up excess milk and had a short life (see Chapter 1), recipes for firm cheeses were designed for longer aging so they could nourish people during the cold winter months, when animals produce less or even no milk. Curing (aging or ripening) firm cheese can take months to years. Some varieties are intended to be consumed as a subtle-tasting young

cheese, but they may also be ripened into a sharp, dry, hard cheese such as Asiago or Gouda.

Many European firm cheeses are governed by specific age criteria; policies on when the cheese is of best quality, or *à point*; and when it should be sold as "seconds" because of dulling flavour, bitterness or other quality degradation. Most firm cheeses in Europe also have an emblem or code placed on them before ripening that notes the production date and place, as a way of monitoring marketplace practices. It's a system we should adopt here.

Over the years I have talked with many cheesemakers frustrated by the additional "aging" and/or abuse their cheeses may be subjected to after they leave the plant.

What's on Your Cheeseboard?

Sue Riedel
Cheese Blogger
cheeseandtoast.com

Cheese Columnist
Globe and Mail

Figaro
Avonlea Clothbound
 Cheddar
Mont-Jacob

They worry because the cheese is no longer what they created from the milk, and fear that consumers may be turned off their cheese if it is eaten past its prime. Too much inventory, lack of a promotion plan, improper packaging, not turning the cheese regularly and poor refrigeration are just a few of the issues that can have a negative effect on a cheese once it's in the marketplace. Good cheesemongers and restaurateurs take proper care of their cheese and sell or serve you only the quality they themselves would purchase. Sometimes cheesemakers sell their cheese as "seconds" because they have to. The cheese may not be what they consider their best effort, but it is in their inventory. You could liken this practice to grocery stores selling day-old bread or overripe produce that's okay but no longer in its prime.

Lovers of Canadian cheese (especially Cheddar and Gouda) should know what they are buying: when it was made, where it was aged, who aged it and in what format— just like soft cheese, firm cheese ripens best in its original size and shape and under certain conditions. There is a market for "extreme" aged Cheddar, but what some brands refer to as "extra-old" would not come close to Canada Grade A standards, even though a premium price may be charged. Specific age guidelines for a cheese should be mandated by cheesemakers because they know their cheese best (as they often are in Europe). This way the arbitrary "longer is better" policy could be abolished.

Several years ago I asked a master cheese grader what

in his experience was the peak age for Cheddar before quality starts to diminish. The answer was three years, with a few exceptional vats of Cheddar lasting beyond that age. He added that additional aging is usually a result of excess inventory (it isn't easy to plan sales so far in advance) or a marketing strategy by some brands to obtain more counter space in stores. I have also posed this question to other makers of fine Cheddar in Canada, and their answer is similar: three years, and sometimes up to five years.

"Protected Denomination of Origin" (PDO) is a quality denominator that has been used in Europe since the 1920s (although AOC or other country-specific designations were used until 1996, when the European Union launched the PDO system). PDO designation is awarded to a product with quality characteristics that are essentially or exclusively a result of its place of origin (climate, nature of the soil, local know-how, and so on). The products must be produced, processed and prepared in a specific region using traditional production methods. The raw materials are strictly defined, such as milk from a specific breed of animal. Roquefort, Parmigiano-Reggiano and blue Stilton, for instance, are PDO cheeses in Europe. The designation is not necessarily a statement of quality, although quality and consistency usually follow the rigorous adherence to criteria used to establish a product's PDO standard.

Heirloom Cheese: The Firm Family

In researching this book, one of the questions I asked of Canadian cheesemongers was "Are there too many of the same cheese being made?" Consistently the answer was no, because there are many twists in cheesemaking that keep them from being the same. I tend to agree, remembering something James Beard experienced when writing his book *Beard on Bread*. He noticed that, although he would give the

Cheese FAQ:
Is there a Canadian cheese PDO?

I believe that some kind of authentic quality differentiation similar to the PDO is in our future, but I am an advocate for extreme caution on the topic. Any program has to be extremely well thought out and have excellent substantiation, or it becomes just marketing hype. Yes, the European program can serve as a model, but don't forget, although the first PDO (then called AOC) was for Roquefort in 1925, the production specifications for Roquefort were enacted as laws 300 years prior! Mastery of product manufacturing was well established, and it was the same with Comte, Beaufort, Brie, Parmigiano Reggiano and all the others!

In this book I've suggested that Tomme de Grosse-Île (page 127) is a potential PDO candidate because the characteristics of the cheese are a result of a specific cow herd being fed foin de batture ("sea hay") from the St. Lawrence River. If it were produced anywhere else or if the cows didn't eat their special grass, the cheese would be different. The methods of gathering the grass, feeding the cows, milking them and making the cheese would all have to be specified in great detail. Cheese or dairy products made from the indigenous pedigree cow of Canada, the Canadienne, have potential for PDO too, if the right criteria are established.

The bigger question is whether there is a benefit to having PDO products. In fall 2013 I spoke with Hervé Mons from Mons Fromager-Affineur about the merits of PDO, because Mons is active in preserving traditional cheesemaking practices, especially the production of cheese using raw milk. Hervé suggested that EU cheese PDOs are just recipes—successful, time-perfected ones that provide consistency, but they are not the only recipes. As much as PDO cheeses have become the cornerstone of great cheese in Europe, there is also an argument

that PDOs have stifled innovation in European cheesemaking, that they are elitist, and have held back the introduction of new cheese because wholesale and retail marketers prefer to stay with the proven assortment.

If the PDO is not a guarantee of quality, do we need it? Will it bring in more revenue for the cheesemaker? Probably not in the short term. Will it benefit the caseophile? They can buy the cheese now. And is there any advantage to such a program at this juncture in Canadian cheese, or would it just serve as a distraction to cheesemakers striving to perfect their cheese and expand their market?

exact same written instructions and the exact same ingredients to his several recipe testers, the results were often different (not bad, just different). That is when he realized how important individual technique is to bread making.

It is exactly the same with cheese, as is evidenced in Somerset County, England, where heirloom clothbound Cheddar is made. The farmstead cheese plants for Keens, Montgomery and Westcombe are within a few miles of each other. The terroir and the animals are similar and they all use raw milk, yet a vertical tasting (done with Jamie Montgomery at the Slow Food Cheese Festival in 2013) of the three same-age clothbound Cheddars these companies produce demonstrated significant differences in the flavour. This is a perfect example of how small twists in plant-specific technique (differences in acidification parameters) can affect the end product.

Heirloom Cheese in This Family

Beaufort (France)

This large (averaging 45 kilograms), round mountain cheese from the French Alps has been famous since Roman times and is made with the raw milk of Tarentaise and Abondance cows. A firm (cooked) washed rind with distinctive concave sides, it has a dense body, buttery texture and a paste colour that has deep golden hues when made in the summer. While Beaufort is wonderful any season, with its fruity aroma and rich nutty and herbal flavours, the summer (*été*) and *chalet d'alpage* versions are superior for their additional floral and herbal tastes. Aging for up to two years concentrates the flavours. Say *bo-for*.

Cave-Aged Gruyère (Switzerland)

Records show that this cheese was being made in 1115 and used as a tithe to local abbeys. The traditional version of this often badly copied cheese is made from raw cow milk, formed in large wheels of up to 40 kilograms and aged in caves for 5 to 24 months. A hard rind, very dense body with few eyes, smooth texture and layered complex flavours of fruit, nuts and hints of musty mushroom, delight the taste buds. The location of the cheese cave in Switzerland, how long it is aged there, and even the *affineur* who does it are marks of quality that delineate Swiss Gruyère cheesemaking. Say *gree-yair*.

 What's on Your Cheeseboard?

Lisa McAlpine and Marla Krisko
Co-owners
Cheese Education Guild

**Five Brothers
Avonlea Clothbound Cheddar
Bleu d'Élizabeth**

Comté (France)

This PDO appellation cheese has been made the same way in the Jura Mountains since the 11th century, from the raw milk of Montbéliard cows. Comté is referred to as the Gruyère of France, with layers of nutty, fruity and sweet toffee flavours, depending on the age (from 6 to 24 months). It is the largest-volume cheese produced in France, made in approximately 250 regional co-operative *fruitières* (small plants) using strict traditional standards. A rigorous 20-point grading program determines whether a wheel of cheese is good enough to be labelled Comté (green label), as well as which wheels are "superior" within the Comté name (red label). Say *com-tay*.

Manchego (Spain)

The best known cheese of Spain and the cheese of Don Quixote in *Don Quixote of La Mancha*, it must be made from the milk of Manchega sheep to be called Manchego (*mahn-chay-go*). Written about in Roman times, Manchego is in danger of becoming a mediocre commodity cheese, as pasteurization and mass production are prolific today. Raw milk Manchego is hard to find, as is any Manchego aged beyond six months. Ideally it is smooth in texture, with nutty, milky, muttony flavours that are zesty on the finish in aged versions. The cheese is highly recognizable by the waxy crisscross pattern on its surface, which used to be created by woven esparto grass.

Montgomery's Clothbound Cheddar (England)

One of the two original producers of English farmhouse Cheddars, the Montgomery family has been making traditional Cheddar in Somerset County for more than three generations. It is handcrafted into 60-pound (27 kg) cloth-wrapped wheels from the raw milk of cows pastured in Somerset. It's a cheese to savour rather than to cook with, so that the many subtle layers of flavour, ranging from sweet grass and nuts to horseradish, can be fully appreciated. The clothbound technique was an innovation prompted by economics. Cheesemakers needed to wrap their product in something that would limit moisture loss as the cheese was aged and allow for formation of a natural protective rind over time. The cloth wrap and a sealing layer of lard were the innovative solutions that also added distinctive flavours.

Handling and Storing Firm Cheese

Air is the enemy of firm cheese because of its low moisture content. Exposure to air dries the cheese, prompts moulding and allows intrusive odours to penetrate cut surfaces. Wrap firm cheese tightly in plastic wrap once it is opened and cut.

Although firm cheeses have long (sometimes 12 months) best-before dates on their precut packages, for best quality I recommend using them soon after purchase and buying fresh cuts of cheese from a cheesemonger on a weekly basis. As with other cheeses, the quality of a firm cheese does not improve after cutting, even if it is vacuum sealed. It's just like fruit: a freshly cut pineapple or melon is much

tastier than fruit cut several days previously. Remember that cheese is alive and fragile, just like produce.

Firm Cheese with Canadian Wine and Beer

Firm cheeses are the most wine friendly. Fruity light, crisp whites, rosés and even sparkling wines go with the younger firm cheeses, while medium- to full-bodied fruit-forward reds such as Meritage, Cabernet Franc or Baco Noir are lovely with the aged versions.

Firm cheese is also very beer friendly, but do consider the type, age and milk in the cheese. A popular pairing is medium and old Cheddar with brown ales, because the smoothness of a cream ale mellows out the spiciness of the cheese. Pilsner, with its dry bitterness, finds a home with mature Cheddar, as do brown beers, dark English ale, Guinness and IPAs—the hoppy bitterness in the beer and the sharpness of the Cheddar smooth each other out. Cloth-bound Cheddars with their nutty flavours and occasional crystals are wonderful with malty beers.

Provolone finds harmony with ales and dark beers, while nutty Gouda and Swiss styles take nicely to ale, especially smooth cream and nut-brown ales with a low hop. With smoked cheese, choose lighter beers such as pale ale or lager that won't compete with the cheese. Sheep milk firm cheeses match well with medium bodied English-style ales.

Ladder of Cheese Appreciation: Firm Cheese

If you like the heirloom cheese on the bottom rung of the ladder, it is likely that you will enjoy the Canadian cheese on the other rungs. It's not that they necessarily taste the same, but they have similar characteristics such as texture and body. The flavours may be more or less similar, depending on the age of the cheese at the time you taste it.

Lindsay Bandaged Cheddar
Canotier de l'Isle
Five Brothers
Aged Farmhouse
Avonlea and/or Farmhouse Clothbound Cheddar
English Clothbound Cheddar

Dairy Farmers of Canada

Cheddar 101

The process for making Cheddar is called cheddaring, a traditional process developed in England, in which the curds are formed into long sheets and stacked to promote the draining of whey. After draining, the curd mass is milled (cut into tiny pieces) and pressed into moulds to extract more whey before the cheese is cured.

Most brands of Cheddar are available from mild to five years old. To really appreciate what aging does to the quality of a cheese, do what the professionals do and have a vertical tasting. Either choose different brands of cheese that are all the same age or explore three to five different ages of one brand. It's common to like one age in one brand and a different age in another, because not all Cheddar ages the same way.

Cheese FAQ: Does firm cheese age in its vacuum package?

The short answer is no—or not the way it's supposed to age. Cheese must be aged under the same conditions that a cheesemaker or professional *affineur* would use, namely conditions of proper humidity, airflow and temperature. The most important factors in aging a firm cheese are to start with a very good quality young cheese and to monitor it regularly during the aging period for appropriate body and flavour development. Typically, the longer a cheese is aged, the more pronounced the flavour will become. Once a cheese has been cut and perhaps vacuum sealed, it is essentially inert and no longer ages (although it still needs refrigeration). Small cuts of cheese are especially affected.

The following guidelines are used by most Cheddar brands for naturally aged Cheddar (time-aged as opposed to enzyme-aged). The only mandated age requirement is for Canadian Aged Cheddar, which must be a minimum of nine months old to use the name.

Cheddar Label	Aging Period
Mild	0 to 3 months
Medium	4 to 6 months
Aged	9 months minimum*
Extra-Old	12 months or longer
Mature	3 to 5 years

* As of December 2008, any Canadian Cheddar labelled "aged" must have a minimum of nine months' age and must be made from 100% whole real milk (milk that hasn't been broken into its individual components) using a process representative of traditional Cheddar. The age of the cheese must be declared on the main label.

Cheese FAQ:
Is organic cheese better?

Not necessarily. Organic farming is a system of farming that maintains and replenishes soil fertility without the use of toxic and persistent synthetic pesticides and fertilizers (see http://www.organicbiologique.ca/en/what.html). Making organic cheese is a positive strategy and practice, but it's not a guarantee of higher cheese quality, especially considering the additional price these cheeses command.

Many cheesemakers and dairy farmers feel that organic regulations overlook some important animal well-being issues. Therefore, instead of "going organic," these cheese processors choose to be part of organizations, such as Local Food Plus in Ontario or the Heritage Dairy Farm Association in British Columbia, that place equal value on land and animal stewardship. Small artisan and farmstead cheesemakers know that when your animals are contented and healthy, they provide better milk, which means taking care of the land the animals graze on. These practices are close to organic without the cost of official certification.

Best Baa Dairy and Ewenity Co-operative members follow the guidelines of Local Food Plus, and they also adhere to the "five freedoms" practised by farming communities in the United Kingdom: (1) freedom from hunger and thirst, (2) freedom from fear and disease, (3) freedom from discomfort, (4) freedom from pain and injury, and (5) freedom to express natural, normal behaviour (for example, lactation cycles). By providing animals with these freedoms, Best Baa and its Ewenity milk suppliers believe their animals tend to be healthier and their need for medication rare. They are committed to production of wholesome milk from healthy, happy ewes. While this practice does not guarantee cheese quality, respect for the animals producing the primary ingredient is assured and suggests that the milk will be transformed into dairy products worthy of the sheep that produced it.

Agropur Grand Cheddar

Agropur
Longueuil, QC

Awarded the title "World's Best Aged Cheddar" numerous times, Grand Cheddar is made from unpasteurized milk using traditional Cheddar methods and naturally aged for one, two, three or five years. It goes through a rigorous production and aging process, under the supervision of master cheesemakers who have honed their crafting of Cheddar for decades in order to strike a balance between flavour and bite. The smooth, creamy texture crumbles with age, offering increased levels of fruity sharpness characteristic of Quebec aged Cheddar.

Avonlea Clothbound Cheddar

Cows Creamery
Charlottetown, PEI

Avonlea

Originally Cheddar was made in large cylindrical wheels that were wrapped in cheesecloth (called a "bandage") and coated with lard. The technique helps to retain moisture and allow formation of a natural protective rind during curing. Cheesemaker Armand Bernard at Cows has revived this tradition, following the style of Orkney Island farmstead Cheddars in Scotland.

Avonlea Clothbound is made from thermized Holstein cow milk that comes from small farms around PEI. It is aged 12 months in carefully monitored temperature and humidity conditions. The earthy aroma, reminiscent of fresh, unwashed potatoes, is unique, due to Prince Edward Island's salt air and iron-rich red soil. The flavour has layers of fruit, roasted nuts and tang on the long finish. Slight moulding around the exterior of the wheel is common in this style of Cheddar and actually contributes to the flavour. It is managed by washing the cheese rind with brine before sending it off to market.

. . . .

The reason for the long-time national success of this truly premium brand is that Balderson has remained true to what it does best—Cheddar—rather than digressing into other types of cheese. It may surprise you to learn that it's made in a very large industrial plant. The secret is careful monitoring and a rigid grading program for any Cheddar bearing the Balderson brand. In 1982 Balderson was first named "World's Best Cheddar." Shortly after that the company established a grading program, through which it has maintained consistent quality and reputation. For nearly 30 years the grading strategy for Balderson brand has essentially been to select the same quality of cheese as would be submitted to a cheese competition, namely a 93-plus Cheddar that has reached its peak in flavour, texture, appearance, aroma and finish for the age of that particular Cheddar.

Balderson Cheddar

Balderson Cheese
Winchester, ON

Balderson

Cheddar Curds

Whether made from cow or goat milk, curds are "hot" across Canada. They are available at most plants that make Cheddar, because curds are actually Cheddar before it is moulded and aged. That said, you can make curds from other firmer cheese styles, but Cheddar is the most preferred. Good curds are made from pasteurized fresh milk because they are sold and best eaten at less than a week old, so they can't be made from thermized or raw milk. And they are best when *really* fresh (not frozen, not vacuum packed). Purveyors of fresh curd get them to stores on Thursday morning with the plan to sell out by Monday, so they are still squeaky (a sign of being fresh). Sure, you can microwave the curds you buy in large stores till they squeak (15 to 20 seconds on medium, or place the curds in warm water), but it's just not the same as factory fresh. An amazing array of tasty curd flavours exist if you want variety. *Upper Canada's Guernsey Curds* are crafted with a vintage mill which produces old fashioned long curds (eliminating 'finds', smaller bits of less desirable curds).

Squeaky Cheese

David Bedouin, a native of Quebec who now lives in British Columbia, saw an opportunity to share his curd experience. In 2005 he founded Squeaky Cheese in collaboration with Village Cheese of Armstrong, BC, where he makes the squeaky curd and then distributes it throughout the Okanagan and Vancouver. Being from Quebec, Bedouin knows a thing or two about cheese Curd and also the decadent, delicious Quebec comfort food poutine (fresh hot french fries and fresh cheese curds topped with spicy warm gravy). He prefers the name "Squeaky Cheese" to "cheese Curds" because it sounds more friendly and funnier, which matches his way of doing business.

· ·

It was a desire to offer a more traditional product that prompted The Farm House to go from waxed wheels of Cheddar to traditional bandaging and coating with lard. Cheesemaker Debra Amrein-Boyes feels that the flavours are more floral and complex than in the same age of her waxed Cheddar (both are made from pasteurized cow milk). At a mere 12 months (the maximum age Debra likes), Farm House Clothbound delivers a rich, smooth body and long layers of flavour ranging from savoury, nutty and sweet to Cheddary sharp.

Squeaky Cheese
Kelowna, BC

NAPAQ

· · · · · · · · · · · · · · · · · ·

Clothbound Cheddar

The Farm House Natural Cheeses
Agassiz, BC

Tasting Notes: Cheddar

Cru du Clocher Cheddar

Le Fromage au Village
Lorrainville, QC

In 1996, husband-and-wife team Hélène Lessard and Christian Barrette followed their dream and changed their life-style by opening their petite Cheddar factory under the big Lorrainville clock tower (*clocher* in French, pronounced *closh-ay*). Winters are long in the Témis-camingue region and Christian's eyes dance when he describes how his cows literally jump for joy when let out of the barn each spring. He says they feast on the grasses as if they know their season in the pasture will be short. Luckily Christian harvests plenty of grass in the summer so he can feed his three herds all winter.

Hélène's use of fresh raw milk in this naturally aged handmade Cheddar promotes flavour development that makes it seem older than its actual age. Premium in quality, this Cheddar has a dense body and typically fruity taste.

Empire Old-Fashioned Cheddar

Empire Cheese and Butter Co-op
Campbellford, ON

This first cheese plant east of Toronto opened its doors in 1870. Empire believes that making cheese the tra-ditional way, in open-style vats, gives it and the fresh curds better flavour. Their aged Cheddars are sharp, fruity and generally creamier than their age indicates. I prefer the younger ones over the mature Cheddar, while the curds sold at the plant provide a trip down memory lane.

Canadian Cheese

Cheese FAQ: What makes a Cheddar Canada Grade 1 quality?

There are pages of criteria. The condensed attributes are:

- The **body** should be of firm, consistent composition, closed and dense, without slits or pinholes in the paste.
- The **colour** should be uniform, not pale or mottled in some sections (although some mature Cheddars may exhibit white specks in the paste).
- The **aroma** should be milky, not yeasty, sour or fruity.
- The **texture** should be smooth to somewhat crumbly in mature Cheddar.
- The **flavour** should be clean (not bitter, overly fruity, barnlike or dirty), with well-developed Cheddar sharpness consistent for its age.

Flavoured Cheddars

One could spend a lifetime trying all the varieties of flavoured Cheddar, let alone write about them! Creativity in flavours, formats and curd styles abound. The golden rule is to start with Canada Grade 1 Cheddar and then use just enough of a high-quality seasoning base. Any age of cheese can be used to create flavoured Cheddar, but mild to medium is most common. While there will always be local and personal favourites, here are a few of my picks:

Tasting Notes: Cheddar

**Caramelized Onion Cheddar
and Thai Curried Cheddar**
Pine River Cheese and
Butter Co-op
Ripley, ON

Maple Cheddar
Black River Cheese
Milford, ON

Île-aux-Grues Cheddar

Fromagerie Île-aux-Grues
Isle-aux-Grues, QC

Caramelized Onion Cheddar and Thai Curried Cheddar

These cheeses are unique because of their marbled curd effect. Curry with Cheddar might sound like a stretch, but it works! And caramelized onions? Well, they're good with just about everything, in my opinion!

Maple Cheddar

This is one of several maple Cheddars produced across the country. Launched as part of Prince Edward County's annual Maple Fest in 2003, it was an instant hit. It is made with pure maple syrup and maple sugar from Prince Edward County. It doesn't get more Canadian than that, eh?

Nonpasteurized (thermized) cow milk from a very specific four-farm region in Isle-aux-Grues, on the St. Lawrence River, contributes to the flavour of this consistently excellent naturally aged Cheddar. Culling the cheese regularly (as winemakers do with their wine) means that only the best Cheddar is aged longer. Look for balance in the layers of clean flavour, from sharp to fruity to salty; and in the five-year-old, notice the characteristic dry body, which has a few protein crystals but a smooth texture.

The cheese factory is the economic

heart of the island, but it can also be said that the factory is in the hearts of the island's inhabitants. With their tenacity, vitality, personal investment and know-how, they have successfully preserved this rich and unique heritage that has united them and sustained them from day to day in their extraordinary island life.

First established in 1888 by a co-operative of local dairy farmers, today Maple Dale is a family-run business. Cheesemaking continues the way it always has, using 100% farm-fresh Canadian milk. They continue to win awards and in 2013 completed their HAACP (Hazard Analysis Critical Control Point) certification, a step that will (among other things) ensure that their tried-and-true cheesemaking process will continue into the future.

Dairy Farmers of Canada

Maple Dale Cheddar

Maple Dale Cheese
Plainfield, ON

Monforte Sheep Milk Cheddar

Monforte Dairy
Stratford, ON

Compared to cow milk Cheddars in the 12 to 18-month-old category, Monforte's Cheddar, made from pasteurized sheep milk, has a distinctly different taste, with intriguing layers of clean nutty, herbal and savoury flavours. It's the only sheep milk Cheddar I know of in Canada, and perhaps the world, because sheep milk is expensive and you need lots of it to make Cheddar (10 kilograms of milk makes just 1 kilogram of cheese) or any firm cheese. Also, there is so much less sheep milk available in Canada than cow milk. Cheesemaker Ruth Klahsen was wise to use the more labour-intensive and costly clothbound technique; the cheese looks so distinctive and, more important, develops mature Cheddar attributes in much less time than block-format Cheddars. Monforte is truly a unique and phenomenal Cheddar experience!

Organic Cheddar

To maintain certified organic status, a cheese plant must abide by the organic rules of the federal and/or local certification group with which the plant is certified. This includes the stipulation that cows must eat primarily grass and be in pasture the maximum amount of time, throughout the warm months (approximately April to November). When cows are in pasture, they eat what they graze on. During the winter months they primarily eat grass that the farmer collects during harvest and stores until needed. They are also fed grains such as alfalfa, peas, oats, soybeans and corn. All their feed must be 100% certified organic, free of synthetic pesticides, fertilizers and GMOs (genetically modified organisms), and must not contain any animal by-products. Ideally, all the feed for the cows is produced on the dairy farm and then the manure is properly composted and recycled back onto the crops. Products bearing the "Organic Canada" label have met the Canadian government's regulatory requirements for organic products (see http://www.organicbiologique.ca). In Quebec, products are certified organic by Québec Vrai, the province's non-profit organic accreditation organization.

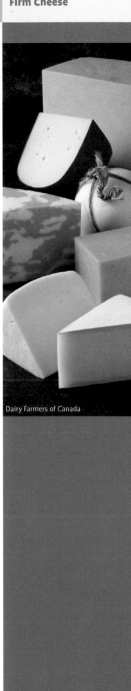

Dairy Farmers of Canada

Organic Cheddar is made in the same manner as non-organic Cheddar except that thermalized organic milk is used. The milk is from family-operated farms and the cheesemaking recipe is rennet-free. It is naturally aged to fully develop the classic Cheddar tastes associated with the various ages. Widely available brands are biobio and L'Ancêtre, from Quebec, and Organic Meadow, a nationally certified organic dairy company hailing from Ontario.

Tasting Notes: Chedda

Perron Cheddar

Fromagerie Perron
Saint-Prime, QC

Since 1890 the Perron family has been exporting Cheddar to England—more than a century, and four generations! Their Cheddars are made in the traditional Canadian way, with thermized fresh milk, the traditional cheddaring process and slow natural aging. The result is a consistently premium Cheddar that has a dense, closed body, a smooth texture and a clean, sharp flavour with characteristic fruitiness. Interesting too is that Perron has a well-designed package—your first indication of the craftsmanship inside!

Smoked Cheddar

Applewood Smoked Cheddar
Cows Creamery
Charlottetown, PEI

Maple Smoked
Extra Old Cheddar
Bothwell Cheese
New Bothwell, MB

Balderson Double Smoked
Balderson Cheese
Winchester, ON

A growing category and an all-Canadian taste, the best versions of smoked Cheddar start with Grade A Cheddar, often aged two years. It is then treated to cool smoke from smouldering wood (pure maple, apple and hickory are common) for various lengths of time, which vary by company. The goal is to produce a full smoky flavour that complements the complex nutty taste of the aged cheese without overpowering it. My recommendations:

- **Applewood Smoked Cheddar**
  (Cows Creamery, Charlottetown, PEI)
- **Maple Smoked Extra Old Cheddar**
  (Bothwell Cheese, New Bothwell, MB)
- **Balderson Double Smoked**
  (Balderson Cheese, Winchester, ON)

Canadian Cheese

Dairy Farmers of Canada

Wilton has been making cheese since 1867 and has a reputation for Cheddar under both the Wilton and Jensen brands. Made from fresh thermized cow milk using the traditional cheddaring process and natural aging, the cheese has the balanced sharp, clean flavour and smooth, slightly crumbly texture that are characteristic of fine aged Ontario Cheddars.

Wilton Cheddar and Jensen Cheddar

Wilton Cheese Factory
Odessa, ON

Dairy Farmers of Canada

Gouda 101

You say *gow-duh* and I say *goo-duh*, while the Dutch say *hhow-duh*. All are understood among caseophiles, who, like the pair in the *tomayto/tomahto* debate, still get along just fine. More important than the pronunciation is to respect this internationally famous cheese with its simple farmhouse origins. Historically speaking, Gouda is a cow milk cheese from the Netherlands aged from several weeks to three and occasionally five years. Gouda is generally aged in a clear wax; it receives the coloured wax coating that differentiates the ages and styles of the cheese before it leaves the factory.

Fortunately, many authentic Gouda cheesemakers have been seduced into making Canada their home, so we can boast the superior (mostly raw milk) Gouda that was originally made in the Netherlands. This is infinitely better than the gummy, dull pasteurized industrial Dutch Gouda common in supermarkets from coast to coast. For anyone who likes Cheddar or Swiss, Gouda is the next delicious rung on the cheese appreciation ladder. There are a number of Canadian Goudas that will please and astound your taste buds. As well, Gouda is one of the more economical artisan cheeses you can buy.

Aged Gouda and Grizzly

Sylvan Star Cheese
Red Deer, AB

The farmstead Gouda from Sylvan Star is made from thermalized cow milk. Only the very best of their Gouda gets aged and/or gains the status of Old Grizzly (page 186). Sylvan Star has been aging Gouda since 1999 and has won awards for every age. Just as with Cheddar, it is interesting to do a vertical tasting to experience the progression of a cheese by the same maker as it ages.

Dairy Farmers of Canada

Aged Premium Dutch

Mountainoak Cheese
New Hamburg, ON

The English translation of the Dutch family name van Bergeijk is "from the mountain oak," hence the name of the dairy farm and the cheese made at this farmstead cheese plant started in 2012. The cheese is Gouda-style, made from the freshest possible pasteurized cow milk just minutes after the last cow in the herd is milked. Premium

Dutch is slightly moister than traditional Dutch Gouda but has the same attributes as regular Gouda. After one year of climate-controlled aging it has a slightly crunchy texture, sweet, nutty flavours and a caramelized finish. My first experience with Mountainoak Cheese was negative: I bought it from a supermarket cheese case where it had been precut two weeks earlier. Perseverance was rewarded when others told me how good this cheese is. The next time, I went to a cheesemonger, who gave me a fresh cut of the cheese. Many cheeses don't get a second chance to prove themselves, and it's not always the cheesemaker's fault.

Eweda Cru

Best Baa Dairy
Fergus, ON

Lait cru is French for "raw milk." Raw milk from British Milk sheep and careful aging for nine months are the keys to the flavour complexity of this cheese, which starts off as a traditional Gouda recipe. Firm but creamy, an earthy aroma leads to explosive, complex flavours that are lactic, sour and nutty at first, then grassy, with lingering sweet butter and fruity notes. It's as beautiful outside as in: kelly-green wax coats the ivory-coloured cheese, reminding the eater of the rolling grassy pastures where the sheep graze. Each 3-kilogram cylinder is marked with information about the producer of the milk used in the cheese;

this creates traceability and accountability for the quality of each wheel.

Regular Eweda, made from pasteurized sheep milk, is aged four to six months and coated in yellow wax. The texture is smooth while the flavour is mildly tart, with the fruitiness of sheep milk. The regular Eweda I had recently was nuttier and more full-flavoured than I remembered—a testimony to Elisabeth's ever-improving skill as a cheesemaker.

Flavoured Gouda

Like Cheddar, flavourings abound in Gouda, with the most popular being the traditional cumin. Here are three of my favourite picks:

Fenugreek Gouda and **Nettle Gouda**
Thunder Oak Cheese Farm
Thunder Bay, ON

Fenugreek Gouda and **Nettle Gouda**
The combination of mild, nutty Gouda and fenugreek, a complex sweet, celery-tasting spice normally used in Indian cooking, raises the bar for flavoured cheese from ordinary to extraordinary. While nettle (often used as a medicinal herb) has a slightly bitter leaf, it contrasts beautifully with three-month Gouda and adds a delightful aromatic to the cheese.

Smoked Onion and Peppercorn Gouda
Island Farmhouse Gouda/
Cheese Lady's Gouda
North Winsloe, PEI

Smoked Onion and Peppercorn Gouda
This is a most pleasant, albeit complicated, spice blend of onion, garlic, peppercorn, pepper flakes, ginger and horseradish in a medium age, judiciously light-smoked Gouda! The

balance of cheese and savoury flavours and the enjoyable lingering of all the tastes is quite amazing.

• •

The 1-kilogram small wheel format of this fine Gouda allows the cheese to develop rich, sweet, nut to herbal flavours and smooth body in only three months (much sooner than larger wheels). This handcrafted Gouda utilizes thermized milk, so it retains much of the flavour of fresh raw cow milk.

• •

Margaret and Jacob Schep moved to Canada in 1981 and started a Holstein dairy cow farm. In 1995 they began making Gouda using an award-winning recipe from Margaret's mother in Holland. Today their son Walter and his wife, Joanne, make the cheese. Part of the reason their Gouda is so distinctive is the gravity-fed milk system (a system widely used by boutique winemakers), which carries the milk to the cheese vat gently, keeping its composition in peak condition. There are several ages and flavours of Thunder Oak farmstead Gouda. Each of the rich, smooth-textured cheeses is naturally aged and has particular savoury to fruity layers of flavour, often with a pleasant toffee finish. The oldest Gouda aged at Thunder Oak is extra old (just over a year), but some Thunder Oak customers age the Gouda longer.

• • • • • • • • • • • • • • • • • • •

Mini Gouda

That Dutchman's Farm
Upper Economy, NS

• • • • • • • • • • • • • • • • • • •

Thunder Oak Gouda

Thunder Oak Cheese Farm
Thunder Bay, ON

Canadian Cheese

Provolone 101

Provolone is a firm pasta filata cheese, which has a stretched or pulled curd (see page 70) formed into a variety of shapes: balls, long salamis and large pear shapes. One pear shape, called *gigantico*, requires upwards of seven months for proper natural aging. Sometimes the enzyme lipase is used in provolone (and other firm Italian-style cheeses) to enhance the smoky aged flavour profile and to make the cheese seem older. If manufacturers use the enzyme judiciously, the cheese won't leave a burning sensation in your throat. When they don't, you'll know. Provolone is often tied with rope, which was traditionally functional for hanging the cheese during curing, transportation and display. The waxy natural rind is usually edible but doesn't add to the flavour of the cheese.

This handcrafted 4-kilogram *piñata* (pear-shaped) provolone is tied with string and hung to age for six months to bring out the smoky nuttiness of an authentic provolone.

Provolone Mezzano Pignata

International Cheese
Toronto, ON

This handcrafted pear-shaped provolone with a waxy natural rind gets its name from the Italian word *dolce*, meaning "mild." Even with only two months of aging this fine pasta filata provolone exhibits a tender curd and a slightly sweet yet piquant taste.

Santa Lucia Sweet Provolone

International Cheese
Toronto, ON

Swiss 101

The country is Switzerland and the cheese is Swiss or Emmental. Gruyère and Swiss-style cheeses are truly among my favourites. When I came to Canada in the 1980s, a lot of the Canadian Swiss cheese available was bitter, elastic and—no surprise—unpopular. Luckily all this has changed and now Swiss cheese with ideal qualities abounds. A good Swiss has a tender though firm body, regularly spaced large eyes (holes), and a sweet to nutty flavour; it should be aged a minimum of 60 days. Two brands that make quality Swiss cheese time after time are:

- **St. Fidèle** (Fromagerie St-Fidèle, La Malbaie, QC)
- **Perron Swiss** (Fromagerie Perron, Saint-Prime, QC)

Cheese FAQ: How does Swiss cheese get its holes?

Contrary to folklore, it's not mice that make the holes in Swiss cheese, but rather a gas produced during ripening by the bacteria culture. The holes are called eyes, and a high quality Swiss cheese should have large, evenly distributed eyes that are nickel to quarter size throughout the body. Swiss cheese with no eyes is said to be "blind."

Aged Farmhouse

Natural Pastures
Courtenay, BC

Low aroma but high in flavour! This fabulous pasteurized cow milk cheese is Boerenkaas carefully aged to bring out a complex cornucopia of flavours that range from nutty to savoury to fruity, ending with caramel and butter notes. It's light buttery in colour and slightly granular but smooth to creamy in texture.

Allegretto

La Vache à Maillotte
La Sarre, QC

This artisan sheep milk cheese owes its distinctiveness to the warm days and cool nights of the Abitibi summer. This releases more sweetness in the grass the sheep feed on. Made from the raw milk of a single flock of sheep, after 120 days of curing the cheese is dry yet smooth, with subtle slightly fruity, distinctly sheep milk flavours.

Blackburn

Fromagerie Blackburn
Jonquière, QC

This is a cheese with minimal aroma but full nonpasteurized cow milk flavour, ranging from sour and salty to sharp, with a lovely slightly bitter vegetal note (could there be nettles in the pasture?). Aged 6 to 12 months, smooth in texture with a thin brushed rind, a taste of Blackburn is an unforgettable cheese experience.

This is a Portuguese version of Cheddar, and likely the cheese that British sailors taught the Portuguese to make when they restocked their ships' larders in the Azores before voyages to the New World. Corvo features a gentle buttery aroma and firm body. It is dry and smooth in texture, with a dense body and a clean, sharp, medium to old Cheddar kick. Try it in a grilled cheese sandwich on rye bread.

Corvo

Portuguese Cheese Company
Toronto, ON

Shep Ysselstein is a relative newcomer to the Ontario artisan cheese scene (since 2011), but you'd never know it by the consistency and overall quality of his cheese. The influence of techniques he learned while making cheese in the Swiss Alps is reflected in both Five Brothers and Handeck (page 185). At this family operation the cow milk arrives at the cheese plant from just a few hundred metres away: Friesvale Farms, a dairy farm started by Shep's grandfather, who emigrated from Holland to Ontario in the 1950s.

The name Five Brothers isn't a coincidence—Shep indeed has five brothers. This handcrafted firm, washed rind cheese combines traits of Gouda with the classic Appenzeller from Switzerland. Natural aging on cedar planks with regular washing and turning for a minimum of eight months develops deep flavour in the cheese. Expect the

Five Brothers

Gunn's Hill Artisan Cheese
Woodstock, ON

delicate aroma of milk, occasional eyes in the body, and a rich, smooth texture with lingering nutty and sweet grassy overtones. In 2014 an 18-month version will be released. I hope Shep has also learned from the Swiss to do his own *affinage* in order to ensure the best representation of his cheese in the market.

Fleurs d'Ail

Le Fromage au Village
Lorrainville, QC

"Firm and unripened" aroused my interest, as did the fact that this pasteurized cow milk cheese uses the milder part of garlic—the flowers (called scapes)—as its key ingredient. This is very creative and different in texture and approach from other flavoured cheeses. Try it crumbled wherever you might use feta. It browns nicely too.

Lankaaster

Glengarry Fine Cheese
Lancaster, ON

Grassy and sweet, with a taste of butter on the finish when it's young, as this cheese ages, more nutty to savoury tastes develop (see Aged Lankaaster, page 184). Made from pasteurized cow milk, this cheese is as addictive as it is versatile. Cheesemaker Margaret Peters says, "Lankaaster is somewhat similar to Gouda, where the curd is washed to give it a pliable closed texture and to reduce acid and lactose production, thus allowing for a more delicate, balanced flavour." The yellow waxed, rounded "loaf" of cheese is unique, meant to be sliced and eaten on bread, as Dutch farmers do.

Canadian Cheese

Two beautiful small hills in the Havre Aubert landscape inspired the cheese dairy to name this cheese. It's made from the thermized milk of one herd of cows whose feed comes from the Magdalen Islands, where they live. This firm pressed, washed and brushed cheese is aged six to eight months. At first a lively lactic aroma, smooth texture and pleasantly fruity taste define the cheese, but then a flavour bursting with lingering sweet nuts and cultured milk follows. A delightful cheese with surprising character!

Tomme des Demoiselles

Fromagerie du Pied-de-Vent
Havre-aux-Maisons, QC

This cheese is styled after an English farmhouse recipe, using raw organic Jersey cow milk. The curd is neither heated nor pressed (unlike other firm cheeses) but left to drain under its own weight. The firm curd forms a crumbly texture that compresses slowly with age. This fine, flaky-textured cheese is long on flavour, with sweetness on the palate and a hint of truffle on the natural rind. Sisters Julia (cheesemaker) and Susan (farm manager) Grace age this cheese no longer than ten months, and they named it after themselves. White Grace is a very wine friendly cheese.

White Grace

Moonstruck Organic Cheese
Salt Spring Island, BC

Hard
Cheese   6

Dairy Farmers of Canada

All You Need to Know about Hard Cheese

Maturity with benefits is the theme here! Hard cheeses were a matter of necessity in the Old World when mountains, harsh winters and no trains, boats or planes kept regions isolated for long periods of the year. In Canada we may have mountains and harsh winters, but we also have a great distribution system. That's the good news. The bad news is that our cheesemakers no longer craft fine grana-style cheeses such as Parmigiano Reggiano, Grana Padano and Sbrinz.

Today the Canadian interpretation of these classic cheeses is industrialized versions made from pasteurized milk, with higher moisture and much less age. Old World grana cheesemakers use copper kettles to cook the curd; these kettles have been used in Europe for centuries but are only now being "tested" by a few cheesemakers in Canada, after being outlawed for years. Another atrocity that occurs with hard cheese is carried out in the name of convenience: pre-grating, further degrading any flavour beyond salt and sawdust. Production of traditional grana-style cheese represents a huge opportunity to displace imported cheese with Canadian.

Most hard family grana cheeses are intentionally made to be consumed as a hard cheese. They are not released until they have reached the proper degree of hardness, usually after 18 to 24 months. The cheesemaking process is arduous, with whey removal being the particular focus. Slow cooking of the curd at high temperatures, pressing and brining the moulded curd mass for several weeks, and/or rubbing the cheeses with salt are but a few of the steps required. Young cheeses are wiped with brine (to fend off unwanted moulds) and turned frequently during the long aging process until they have a dry, granular body with the characteristic white crystalline specks called *grana*, the signature of age and quality in a hard cheese.

Cheeses such as two-year Gouda and mature three to five-year Cheddars can also develop crystals with age, but they are not considered grana cheeses because they are made using different cheesemaking processes than a hard cheese. Note that crystals can be a defect in cheeses that are too young or in varieties where they don't belong.

Besides high temperature cooking, another way a cheese becomes a hard cheese is through extended aging to dry it out. The moisture level must be 20% to 40% to call it a hard cheese. Asiago, Toscano and Gouda are examples of firm cheeses that age into fine hard cheeses with vigilant nurturing in the proper temperature, humidity and air flow conditions. In other words, you can't age just any old cheese in any old fridge; you have to plan for it and guide the cheese into a hard old age.

Cheese FAQ: What are those crunchy bits in my cheese?

Grana crystals are actually tyrosine, formed by the natural breakdown of milk protein, which also causes these cheeses to digest quickly—a feature popular with athletes who want a quick protein boost. Hard cheeses have the lowest moisture level of all cheeses, and a higher protein and calcium content, because the milk in them is very concentrated. As well, aged hard cheeses are completely lactose-free because the milk sugar (lactose) is removed with the whey during cheesemaking.

Cheese FAQ: What does salt do in cheesemaking?

Salt is a necessary ingredient in cheese. It adds flavour, arrests the action of lactic acid bacteria when the right level of fermentation is achieved, suppresses spoilage bacteria, and assists in the ripening of cheese. It can be added to the curd, used in a heavy brine solution, or rubbed on the rind. Without salt, cheese would mould very easily and the texture would be greatly affected.

Heirloom Cheese: The Hard Family

At the Slow Food Cheese Festival in September 2009 and again in 2013, I found it very interesting that many issues in Europe are the same as here: pastures for grazing versus urban sprawl or recreational development (ski resorts threaten the demise of mountain *alpage* cheese); safe parameters for selling raw milk; concerns regarding the demise of raw milk cheese production for export to the United States (and, by association, Canada); getting people to eat locally produced food; and encouraging families to cook and eat together. Surprising too is that consumer education about cheese is considered a priority as indus-trial cheese makes its way into the households of younger consumers who lack appreciation for traditional artisan products. Cheesemakers in workshops I went to said that organic accreditation was less important to them than animal welfare, because casein content (milk protein for cheesemaking) is the ultimate measure of milk quality. Only happy, healthy animals have high levels of it. We may be an ocean apart, but our concerns are all too similar.

Heirloom Cheese in This Family

Asiago (Italy)

The popular industrial versions of Asiago bear little resemblance to the traditional cheese, which is more than a thousand years old. Like Cheddar, Asiago is marketed by age because of the dramatic changes that occur in both texture and taste as it ages. Young (*mezzano*) three-month Asiago is mild and milky to sweet in flavour, whereas aged two-year Asiago (*stravecchio*) is sharp and pungent.

Parmigiano Reggiano (Italy)

This is perhaps the most guarded of all cheese quality designations, yet there are still variations at retail. The best quality of this PDO cheese is made from raw summer milk, has ivory to straw-coloured paste with small grana crystals, a fragrant aroma and complex layers of sweet nut, cream, grass and fruit (pineapple) flavours. Its minimum age is 18 months and the most common age is 30 months, with a few of the very best wheels selected for aging three to four years by the Parmigiano Consortium, which governs all aspects of the cheese from cow welfare to cheesemaking and maturation to marketing.

Pecorino Romano (Italy)

Pecorino ("sheep milk cheese" in Italian) is an ancient cheese that has existed for more than two millennia—it was a staple of the Roman legions. The aged version of this PDO cheese is firm to hard to flaky, with salty, fruity and piquant flavours that escalate with age. Pecorino Romano made in Tuscany is called Toscano Romano.

Piave (Italy)

The fertile valley around the Piave River in northeast Italy, where the cows graze and their milk is collected, gives Piave its unique flavour. This firm to hard cheese is made in one dairy co-operative from pasteurized milk. The rind is imprinted with its name. A mature (*vecchio*) Piave is an irresistible interplay of sweet, salty and toasted nut flavours. One of the newer heirloom cheeses, Piave was created in the 1960s to resemble a younger version of Parmesan. Say *pee-ah-vay*.

Handling and Storing Hard Cheese

Low moisture gives hard cheeses a long best-before life. Additional aging at home, however, is not recommended. Once the cheese has been cut and vacuum packed it does not age properly (if at all). Once you've opened it, rewrap the cut piece tightly in plastic wrap and/or a self-sealing plastic bag to keep the air out. Replace the wrap every time you open the cheese. With proper care, you can keep these cheeses in prime condition for several weeks.

Hard cheeses are ideal for grating. However, do it just before using, if at all possible, as flavour is lost very quickly once grated. Prove this to yourself: taste freshly grated grana cheese alongside cheese grated three days and one week before. Store any excess grated cheese in a heavy plastic self-sealing bag with the air removed.

Hard Cheese with Canadian Wine and Beer

For this group it all depends on the type of cheese. Spicy Gewürztraminer goes well with aged Gouda; fruity, well-rounded Merlot or Cabernet Sauvignon with Asiago; and a big Meritage with five-year-old Cheddar or pepato.

Hard cheese is surprisingly good matched with a dark beer. Aged Gouda, with its nutty butterscotch flavours and crystalline crunch, is wonderful with super-malty bigger beers.

Ladder of Cheese Appreciation: Hard Cheese

If you like the heirloom cheese on the bottom rung of the ladder, it is likely that you will enjoy the Canadian cheese on the other rungs. It's not that they necessarily taste the same, but they have similar characteristics such as texture and body. The flavours may be more or less similar, depending on the age of the cheese at the time you taste it.

Old Grizzly

Aged Lankaaster

Toscano

Handeck

Tania Toscana

Italian Piave

Aged Lankaaster

Glengarry Fine Cheese
Lancaster, ON

Some of Glengarry's Lankaaster loaves (page 174) remain in the aging room for 14 to 24 months to develop intense yet balanced layers of caramel, butterscotch, pineapple and butter flavours that linger and linger on the palate. During this time, the body goes from semi-firm to hard without losing its overall smoothness in texture. In late 2013 Aged Lankaaster won "Global Supreme Champion" at the Global Cheese Making Competition in Somerset, England, out of 167 categories. So expect this awesome cheese to be in short supply for a couple of years until the magic of aging transforms a simple but beautiful cheese into a masterpiece. And then be sure to savour every morsel!

Margaret Peters, owner and cheesemaker at Glengarry, is living her dream of making artisan cheese on a farm in the county where she grew up. This reality grew out of a company she started in 1995, Glengarry Cheesemaking Supply, which provides technical support for farmstead cheesemakers and sells equipment and supplies for farmstead and artisan cheesemaking. Over the years Glengarry has developed recipes with many artisan companies as well as their own.

This simple cooked Romanello-style cheese turns rich and mysterious with a few months of aging and the addition of peppercorns to the cheese curd. It has a firm body and dry texture, yet is creamy, with a lingering sharp taste and a snap of spice.

Aged Pepato

International Cheese
Toronto, ON

There are many bad clones of the classic Italian Asiago, but Thornloe's is a winner with a firm to hard body and black wax coating. At four to five months the characteristic tang is there, but it manages not to overwhelm the more subtle nutty to fruity nuances. One year of controlled aging brings out magnificence in this cheese.

Asiago

Thornloe Cheese
Thornloe, ON

With its large (20-kilogram) wheel format, rustic ochre rind and intensely earthy, musty aroma, Handeck is a cheese that stands out from the rest. The unusually smooth texture of this firm cheese garners a few protein granules along the way and delivers whopping big tastes of roasted nuts, savoury herbs and earthy vegetables. It's produced using the same methods as a typical Swiss mountain-style cheese (cooked and pressed to expel whey), then hand washed, brushed and

Handeck

Gunn's Hill Artisan Cheese
Woodstock, ON

turned for a minimum of 12 months while aging on cedar wood planks (in caves precisely controlled for airflow, temperature and humidity) to bring out the robust flavours. One might think the cheese is made from raw or unpasteurized milk, but it's the bacterial culture, use of traditional rennet and the TLC of its producer, Shep Ysselstein, that makes this cheese a masterpiece. In 2015, look for a two to three-year old version of Handeck. It's nice to have a fine Canadian hard cheese that's other than Gouda or Italian in style.

Old Grizzly

Sylvan Star Cheese
Red Deer, AB

Dairy Farmers of Canada

The farmhouse Gouda from Sylvan Star Cheese comes in six ages. The oldest and most renowned is Old Grizzly. The real McCoy, it's made from thermalized cow milk and aged on site for 12 to 15 months. (A few cheesemongers buy the cheese young and age it themselves, but the result isn't the same as when Sylvan Star's owners, the Schalkwijk family, do it.) As the young Gouda matures into Grizzly, the texture becomes more brittle and the flavour full and sharp, with dried fruit and toffee notes that can linger . . . for hours. Truly a cheese to be sucked slowly, with full attention to the flavour notes.

Tania Toscana Sheep Milk Cheese

Lenberg Farms Classic Reserve
Lindsay, ON

Tania, a Lenberg Farms Toscana sheep, proudly lent her name to this superb cheese, which tends to remind me of Italian Piave, made from pasteurized cow milk. The first sheep herd was added to Lenberg Farms' animal family in early 2011, and they have wasted no time in making a truly brilliant product with the milk.

After cheese curd is made from pasteurized Ontario sheep milk, it is pressed into cloth-lined wheel moulds and set to cure on pine slabs, with frequent turning and washing, for a minimum of six months. The result is beautifully well-rounded, lingering sweet and nutty flavours. But waiting beyond six months is even more rewarding! As the curd gets drier (though still rich and moist) the flavours become more concentrated, with definite caramel and smoky notes towards the rind, while the paste becomes an attractive tan colour (again like Piave). Now, you may think that description sounds like aged Gouda, but the flavour differences are considerable. What an interesting comparison it would make to serve a one to two-year old Gouda, a bandaged Cheddar and Tania Toscana together!

As a side note, my first experience with this cheese was a tragedy. I bought a pre-wrapped cut at the cheese counter of a reputable supermarket. The cheese was dull (low in flavour) and

Tasting Notes

dry, with barely detectable roasted nut flavours. It had been wrapped in the plastic for three weeks. Had I been a normal customer I probably would not have tried the cheese again. However, knowing the awards this cheese had garnered and the quality reputation of its maker, I bought my next sample freshly cut from a cheesemonger. The lesson: precutting and wrapping in plastic for more than a few days can destroy a normally wonderful cheese!

Toscano

Monforte Dairy
Stratford, ON

Sheep milk from Ontario Mennonite shepherds is the start of this cheese that's patterned after Tomme de Savoie, although the name and even the taste are more reminiscent of fine aged Pecorino Toscano from Italy. Hard, dry and earthy, with hints of rosemary, after six months of aging, it's a beautiful cheese to savour.

How to Identify a Good Cheesemonger

This Cheese Education Guild class project is always popular and often enlightening for any cheesemongers in the group. Here are some observations that students have compiled over the years. And yes, there are Canadian cheesemongers from coast to coast who fit the description:

A good cheesemonger . . .

. . . respects and understands cheese, as shown by the way it is displayed and wrapped at the cheese counter as well as how it is packaged for taking home.

. . . feels that à point quality in cheese selections is more important than the number of cheeses carried.

. . . has staff that are friendly, knowledgeable and unintimidating.

. . . knows my preferences as a regular customer but makes suggestions regarding what is à point, in season and/or particularly wonderful of late.

. . . calls or emails me when a particular favourite on my list arrives.

. . . lets me taste cheese before I buy (with the exception of cheese packaged in small formats).

. . . cuts cheese as it is ordered or has a short (three to five days) "packed on" date policy for precut cheese.

. . . offers promotions that make cheese fun while introducing new varieties.

. . . carries cheese books, cheeseboards, serving tools and accompaniments for sale and/or reference.

. . . uses informative signs and tasting notes in the store or makes them available on a website.

. . . can explain why a cheese is expensive—for example, because of hand washing, long aging, a particular crafting technique, type of milk, and so on.

. . . practises fair pricing, knowing that price is less important than service and quality to their customers.

MAPAQ

Blue Cheese 7

Dairy Farmers of Canada

All You Need to Know about Blue Cheese

Love 'em or hate 'em, blue cheeses are anything but ordinary. They can be found in a number of families but most notably in the soft and semi-soft ones. The distinctive difference I find in Canadian blue cheese is the initial sweet note, a prelude to glorious achievement of the anticipated piquant finish. This is so universal in the family that I have to believe it comes from our Canadian soil, which influences the milk.

The common feature among blue cheeses is the visible veins of blue-green or grey mould distributed throughout the cheese. How do those veins get into the cheese? During cheesemaking, the bacteria culture *Penicillium roqueforti* is added to the cheesemilk. After approximately one week, needles are used to pierce the young wheels of cheese, aerating them so the blue mould can grow inside (kind of like aerating your lawn for healthier growth). The veins grow along the needle tracks and then into the cheese. If piercing isn't done, the piquant blue flavour is more subtle, with no vein development.

Sadly, more people are afraid of blue cheese than any other type, usually because of bad experiences with strong styles from Europe. Canadian blues are complex, and most won't knock your socks off. Here are a couple of tips if you are willing but hesitant:

- First, try it cold from the fridge, because cold cheese has less flavour. A Cheese Education Guild student who was a sommelier but very new to cheese confessed that this was how she tasted almost all of our samples during the eight-week course—until she realized she actually liked the cheese!
- Second, because blue cheese ripens from the inside to the outside, the interior and the veins will have a more

pronounced flavour. So taste the non-veined outside edges first, moving to the veined interior only when you are ready.

I've seen many people end up appreciating blue cheese using these tasting methods.

Heirloom Cheese: The Blue Family

A question that has been debated in New World cheese circles for years is whether it helps or hinders cheese recognition to say that a cheese is like an Old World cheese. I tend to think that because cheese is so diverse in flavour and style and people generally know so little about it, they need a point of reference. But then again, some cheeses are so distinctive they don't need or don't really equate to a European original (I call these "Canadian originals" in this book).

Once people understand cheese as well as they understand wine, beer or other gourmet foods, we can let the cheese stand on its own merits of description by cheese family, by maker or by the factory it comes from. A mindset holding us back in Canada (particularly outside Quebec) is that cheese is often considered an accessory to food, something you use in a recipe, or worse yet, an indulgence. In Europe, cheese is food—a main source of protein.

Heirloom Cheese in This Family

Roquefort (France)

Both Caesar and Charlemagne were fans of Roquefort or its kin, and production has been recorded for more than 2,000 years. PDO rules stipulate that any cheese called Roquefort be made from raw sheep milk, produced in a precise geographic region and be ripened in the caves of Mount Combalou at least three months. The result is a creamy balance of rich, spicy, tart to fruity flavours that should not be overly salty or bitter. Say *rohk-for*.

Stilton (England)

Often called "the king of English cheese" and possibly the most requested blue cheese in the world, not all Stilton is created equal. Making the cheese from pasteurized cow milk within a geographic region in central England, using specific traditional ladling methods, creates the perfect PDO Stilton, with a pale yellow cheese curd, deep blue veining and a yeasty aroma. It is firm yet incredibly moist, smooth and creamy, melting on the palate with symmetry of salty, rich, buttery flavours immersed in an overall spiciness that is strong and full, but not overpowering.

Handling and Storing Blue Cheese

Keep air out by wrapping the cheese in foil or plastic wrap, then place it in a self-sealing bag or an airtight container. It is very important to keep blues away from other cheese to avoid mould transfer. Always have a separate knife on the cheeseboard for serving blues. Better yet, give blue its own plate and serving knife. A knife used for blue cheese or the blue's proximity to the other cheeses on a cheese board is often enough to overpower the other selections and taint their flavour and enjoyment.

Blue Cheese with Canadian Wine and Beer

While port is the traditional wine choice for blue cheese, it takes a back seat to our famous Canadian icewines, fruit ciders and late-harvest wines. These sweet yet acid wines provide contrast to the salty blue tang. Nonetheless, fruit-forward reds such as Cabernet Franc and Gamay are my house favourites with blue cheese, as they challenge and stand up to most blues.

Fruit beers, sweet stouts and porters make fabulous pairs with blue cheese. Stout and porter have malt sweetness and buttery tastes, with hints of bitter chocolate, roasted coffee and licorice.

Ladder of Cheese Appreciation: Blue Cheese

If you like the heirloom cheese on the bottom rung of the ladder, it is likely you will like the Canadian cheese on the other rungs. It's not that they necessarily taste the same, but that they have similar characteristics (e.g. texture, body). The flavours may be more or less similar depending on the age of the cheese you have at the time you taste it.

- Ciel de Charlevoix
- Étoile Bleue de Saint-Rémi
- Highland Blue
- Rassembleu
- Country Blue
- English Farmhouse Stilton

Tasting Notes

Baby Blue

Moonstruck Organic Cheese
Salt Spring Island, BC

This small surface ripened blue cheese has a white to blue-grey exterior, depending on its age. It's made from the fragrant pasteurized organic milk of purebred Jersey cows. While the other blues made by Moonstruck are bold and piquant, the addition of *Penicillium roqueforti* to a buttery Brie-style cheese softens the blue tang. Ready to enjoy in three weeks, the flavours develop much more depth (tang as well as complexity) after six to eight weeks.

Bleu Bénédictin

Abbaye Saint-Benoît
St-Benoît-du-Lac, QC

Made by monks at a Benedictine abbey from pasteurized whole cow milk, this premium semi-soft blue is aged at least three months to develop an earthy mushroom aroma; a rich, extra-creamy texture; and complex, pleasantly piquant, lingering flavours.

Heaven on a Plate

Grilled cheese is one of the ultimate comfort foods. I was introduced to my very favourite grilled cheese sandwich at Zees Grill in Niagara-on-the-Lake, Ontario, where I was served grilled Bleu Bénédictin with freshly sliced in-season tomato on thinly sliced toasted focaccia. If you love blue cheese, this is nirvana. It works with any semi-soft Canadian blue.

Le Bleu

Fromagerie La Moutonnière
Ste-Hélène-de-Chester, QC

This distinctive award-winning blue offers the epitome of zesty blue piquancy and salt flavour balance while allowing other, more subtle sweet, grassy cheese flavours to shine through. Lucille Giroux at La Moutonnière uses only traditional rennet when making cheese. She feels that happy sheep, which graze freely, drink natural spring water and take shade as needed under the maple trees in summer, are the essence of her fine cheese.

Bleu d'Élizabeth

Fromagerie du Presbytère
Sainte-Élizabeth-de-Warwick, QC

Every day, milk arrives at this *fromagerie* from a farm where cows feast on clover, timothy grass, bluegrass and other organic grains from certified organic pastures. This farmstead cheese is made from thermalized milk. It has a dense curd with well-distributed greenish veins of *Penicillium roqueforti* obtained during 60 days of curing. Although it can be crumbly (thus difficult to serve neatly), the cheese is ultra-creamy—and neatness is not what counts here. The flavour, initially sweet with balanced salt and a piquant, never bitter finish, is impeccable. The name (pronounced *bloo deh-lisabet*) refers to the town and the former rectory where the cheese is made.

Tasting Notes

Celtic Bleu

Glengarry Fine Cheese
Lancaster, ON

Fruity yet zesty, with a buttery aroma and a balanced salt level, this creamy, rich semi-soft blue has an unusual limestone-coloured natural rind, developed with specific ripening cultures. It's made from pasteurized Brown Swiss and Holstein cow milk; the culture *Penicillium roqueforti* is added to the cheesemilk to create a blue taste that is piquant but not aggressive. Needle lines where the cheese has been pierced allow blue mould to grow and add to the visual interest of the cheese.

Ciel de Charlevoix

**Maison d'Affinage
Maurice Dufour**
Baie-Saint-Paul, QC

The name (pronounced *see-ell duh shar-luh-vwa*) is inspired by the cloud-dotted blue skies of the Charlevoix region. This artisan cow milk blue has a grey natural rind and is aged 60 days to develop complexity. A musty mushroom aroma, ultra-creamy texture and full, lingering blue flavour with hints of salt define this cheese.

Country Blue

**The Farm House
Natural Cheeses**
Agassiz, BC

Debra Amrein-Boyes calls this a Stilton-style blue, and right she is. While others may also use the name of an Old World cheese, some abuse the comparison, missing the mark by miles, which does neither cheese justice. This outstanding firm but creamy blue is piquant and not acid, with deep roasted nut flavours like Cheddar and a perfect salt balance. It is made in a traditional English farmhouse style in which the young cheese curd is not pressed, allowing the blue mottling to develop naturally and thoroughly throughout the paste without piercing. The rind is natural and rustic in appearance, like Stilton. Truly an amazing blue based on a classic, with Canadian authenticity!

. . . .

While this is not a traditional Canadian blue by definition, it certainly is the most novel, in both appearance and name! Enrobed in thick black wax (which makes a handy serving bowl), tangy blue flavour waits inside the soft, buttery cheese, with blue mould appearing only after the cheese is cut. Fans of the cheese recommend that you slice the top off, stir the cheese gently, replace the wax cover and then wait a few days until blue mould is evident. If you live in Ontario you can substitute Devil's Rock, from Thornloe Cheese— similar black wax format, varying creaminess and a nice blue flavour.

. . . .

Dragon's Breath

That Dutchman's Farm
Upper Economy, NS

Tasting Notes

Ermite

Abbaye Saint-Benoît
St-Benoît-du-Lac, QC

Since 1943 the monks at this Bene-dictine abbey on the shores of Lake Memphrémagog have made a living by making cheese. Ermite (meaning "hermit") is made from pasteurized whole cow milk. This semi-soft blue is essentially a young version of Bleu Bénédictin (page 196). With only one month of aging, the Ermite has no rind, is less creamy and has a sharp rather than complex flavour. It's perfect for cooking and for garnishing steaks or burgers.

Étoile Bleue de Saint-Rémi

Fromagerie du Charme
Saint-Rémi-de-Tingwick, QC

Wrapped in blue foil and made from 100% thermized sheep milk, this cheese is reminiscent of Roquefort with its lovely veins of blue-green mould, but is less salty. The flavour sensation starts off meek, moves into sweet and winey and ends with a medium-sharp tang. The taste and creamy texture will please both novice and experienced blue fans.

Geai Bleu

Bergerie aux Quatre Vents
Sainte-Marie-de-Kent, NB

Named for the many colourful blue jays of the region, this blue cheese (pronounced *jzhay bluh*) is made from unpasteurized cow milk and aged a minimum of 60 days. It is exceptionally creamy and pleasingly piquant, exhib-iting the rich, earthy flavours of milk influenced by the salty New Brunswick ocean air. The rind is a rustic ochre colour, almost as if it has been washed with brine.

Move over, Roquefort and Stilton! This handcrafted blue cheese made from raw East Friesian sheep milk is exquisite. Its layers of flavour include tangy blue with slightly salty, sweet, apple butter and wine notes. The paste is ivory coloured with blue-grey veins and is enrobed in an appealing rustic nubbly rind. Aging for a minimum of 60 days develops aromas of wet slate and herbs (especially sage), a smooth body and a rich, earthy blue flavour with less salt and acidity than many blues. For a locavore treat, drizzle lightly with Lanark County maple syrup.

Highland Blue

Back Forty Artisan Cheese
Lanark, ON

Located at the gateway to the picturesque Naramata Bench, this handcrafted blue by Shana Miller uses the pasteurized milk of D Dutchmen Dairy in Sicamous, British Columbia. King Cole is a creamy semi-soft blue that is bold and full-flavoured, with hints of fruity pear or apple. The rustic natural exterior has deep charcoal hues.

King Cole Blue

Upper Bench Winery and Creamery
Penticton, BC

Blue Cheese

Tasting Notes

Rassembleu

**Fromagiers
de la Table Ronde**
Sainte-Sophie, QC

While most blue cheeses are semi-soft and creamy, Rassembleu (pronounced *ra-som-bluh*) has a firm body and natural rind, a woodsy aroma, and flavours of mushroom and caramel. Made from pasteurized organic cow milk and aged 60 to 90 days, its blue notes are subtle and lingering. Perfect for the person new to blue, yet a rare treat too for the blue cheese aficionado.

MAPAQ

Tiger Blue

Poplar Grove Cheese
Penticton, BC

Definitely a blue with some teeth! Richly veined, with a vigorous bite, it's a favourite with the stalwart blue crowd. Tiger Blue's intense flavour and abundant veining—the appearance is more blue marbled than veiny—develop as it matures in Poplar Grove's "blue room," where it's flipped and pierced weekly for five weeks before being wrapped (most blue cheeses are pierced only one time).

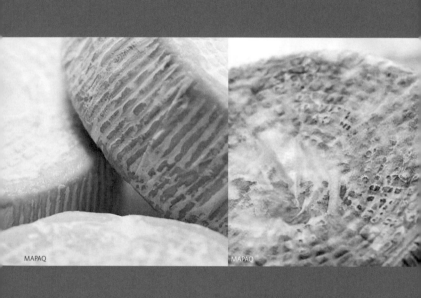
MAPAQ

MAPAQ

Goat Cheese 8

MAPAQ

All You Need to Know about Goat Cheese

The goat has been called the poor man's cow. Goats require less capital to purchase, and their ability to adapt to any environment and to consume almost any kind of plant with a minimum of land make them a versatile farming resource. Unlike cows and sheep, goats don't graze on grass and clover in pastures; rather, they "browse," eating leaves, bark, twigs, shrubs and vines. As with cows and sheep, certain breeds of goat are better than others for producing quality and quantity of milk for cheesemaking. To highlight the cheese from this important milk, they are grouped together in a family, as is done in France.

Many Canadian goat cheeses are suitable for vegetarians, meaning they are made using microbial enzymes rather than animal rennet. However, do read the ingredient label carefully, because ripened varieties modelled on heirloom styles will most likely use rennet to duplicate the curd attributes of the original cheese.

The attributes of cheese made from goat milk change by cheese family in exactly the same manner as cow or sheep milk cheese across the families. In other words, the more moisture there is in the cheese (goat or other milk), the softer it is and the more perishable it will be; that is, it has a shorter à point life. (See Appendix B, "The Significance of Moisture Level," page 226.) A clue that a cheese is made from goat milk is its pure white colour. Goat milk has no carotene; thus the milk lacks the warm ivory, buttery hues of cow or sheep milk. As a goat cheese ages, it will grey slightly from its younger, pure white colour.

You will see from the cheese in this chapter that there is

Cheese FAQ:
Is all goat cheese chèvre?

In North America, chèvre is a fresh cheese made from goat milk. However, in the rest of the world, *chèvre* is actually a French word borrowed from the term *pur chèvre*, which means "made from 100% goat milk." Our 'chèvre' should actually be called *fromage frais* (fresh cheese) made from goat milk. That said, a well-made fresh chèvre is the perfect place to start exploring goat cheese. If you haven't tried fresh chèvre lately, taste it again—you may be surprised. The owners of goat dairies have learned that clean animal teats make for better-tasting, higher-quality cheesemilk. This yields a cheese with a gentler caprine (goaty) flavour, making it acceptable to more customers.

a wide range of goat cheese to explore. Limiting yourself to chèvre would be nothing short of a tragedy, especially when some of the world's best goat cheeses (judged by both award achievement and comparison to heirloom models) are made right here in our own Canadian backyard!

Heirloom Cheese:
The Goat Family

France is king when it comes to soft goat cheese, with the Loire Valley being perhaps the most famous goat cheese region in the world, with a pedigree dating back to the eighth century. Loire goats are not typical browsers: the foliage they ingest is carefully orchestrated to produce cheesemilk of a consistent quality and flavour profile. A high quality goat cheese is defined by its lingering scent

MAPAQ

and aftertaste, and the rind is meant to be eaten, as it reflects the true taste of the cheese.

Traditional PDO recipes (not only for goat cheese) have standards specifying that the milk must go from the animal into the vat within a few hours. Many times starter culture is added to the raw milk the night before cheesemaking, so that while the milk is resting, acidification occurs—this is what is meant by "slow fermentation." The heirloom cheeses below all have PDO status.

Heirloom Cheese in This Family

Chabichou du Poitou (France)

Poitou is the most important goat-breeding region in France and home to many goat milk cheeses. Chabichou is a tiny drum-shaped cheese covered in a thin, wrinkly rind. It has a chalky white paste and a delicate and slightly sweet flavour, with little salt and faint acidity. The best goat cheese is available from April through November.

Sainte-Maure de Touraine (France)

This ancient soft goat cheese from the Loire is known for the straw running through the centre of its 14-centimetre cylinder shape. The straw (pasteurized versions use a stick) is a means to aerate the paste for even ripening and to help the soft young cheese maintain its shape. Considered the most flavourful of the Loire goat cheeses, Sainte-Maure has a bright goat milk tang when young and complex acidic to peppery flavours when mature. (Say *saint-mohre duh too-rain*).

Valençay (France)

This cheese was once produced as a perfect pyramid, but Napoleon chopped off the top with his sword because he did not want to be reminded of Egypt (where he had been defeated). The resulting trapezoid shape continues to be used, as does the moist, dense paste with a melting texture, nutty aroma and balance of lemony goat milk and salt tastes. As you might expect, this cheese is best when made with raw goat milk.

Handling and Storing Goat Cheese

Tiny spots of blue or grey mould can be found on the nubby rinds of many soft, lactic ripened goat cheese styles, so don't rely on appearances when buying or storing these cheeses. Do, however, consider how the cheese is being merchandised before you buy it. These tiny cheeses love air, and because they are small they suffocate quickly when wrapped in plastic. Always unwrap soft ripened goat cheese when you get it home. Place it, unwrapped, in a plastic tub with air left in the container, to allow the cheese to breathe. The paste of lactic ripened goat cheese is slightly firm at first, then moist, dense and almost claylike as it melts in the mouth.

What's on Your Cheeseboard?

Yannick Achim
Owner/Cheesemonger
Yannick Fromagerie, Montréal,
Saint-Jérôme and Québec, QC

Chèvre à ma Manière
Tomme à Rudy
Hercule

Firmer goat cheeses should be handled in the same manner as cheese from other families. As always, buy and enjoy only what you can use in a week or two, for the best flavour representation.

Capricorn View Farms

Goat Cheese with Canadian Wine and Beer

The higher proportion of caproic, caprylic and capric acids in goat milk gives fresh and soft goat cheese a slightly tart, lemony bright taste. These cheeses have a natural affinity for drier crisp white wines such as Sauvignon Blanc, unoaked Chardonnay, Chenin Blanc and any brut Champagne-method bubbly. Firmer goat milk cheeses pair more easily with wine, preferring fuller bodied whites such as Chardonnay, fruity reds (try Zinfandel or Merlot) or a nutty sherry.

What's on Your Cheeseboard?

Ian Picard
Master Cheesemonger
Fromagerie Hamel, Montréal, QC

Chèvre à ma Manière
Gaulois de Portneuf
Bleu d'Élizabeth

Wheat beers pair beautifully with goat cheeses such as chèvre and lactic ripened varieties. The citrusy aspect of wheat beer plays well with the tartness of the cheese, and the high effervescence of the beer is a foil for the sticky fresh paste. Light, mild fruity ales as well as sour beers complement bright, citrusy goat milk cheese.

Ladder of Cheese Appreciation: Goat Cheese

If you like the heirloom cheese on the bottom rung of the ladder, it is likely that you will enjoy the Canadian cheese on the other rungs. It's not that they necessarily taste the same, but they have similar characteristics such as texture and body. The flavours may be more or less similar, depending on the age of the cheese at the time you taste it.

Grey Owl
Pyramid
Chèvre à ma Manière
Sabot de Blanchette
Paillot de Chèvre
French Sainte-Maure or Valençay

Tasting Notes

Blue Juliette

Salt Spring Island Cheese
Salt Spring Island, BC

David Wood, creator of this cheese, gets ten out of ten for this lovely soft disk of pasteurized goat milk curd. A thin bloomy rind laced with blue-grey mould ups the flavour a notch towards piquant without overpowering the delicate mushroom aroma and taste. Kept in proper conditions, Blue Juliette is marvellous eaten near or just after its best-before date. Placing the cheese in a plastic tub at home allows it to breathe and fends off any bitterness.

MAPAQ

Celebrity Chèvre

Mariposa Dairy
Lindsay, ON

In 1989, cheesemaking using the milk from their goat farm was an intense labour of love for husband and wife team Bruce and Sharon Vandenberg. Today Mariposa is a thriving 65-person operation, thanks to a partnership with marketer Finica Foods Specialties, which markets Mariposa cheese under the Celebrity and Lenberg Farms brands across North America. The local economy benefits greatly from Mariposa

Dairy: for every three dollars in sales, two dollars stays in the Kawartha community. My favourite picks:

- **Cranberry Cinnamon Log**, a hand-rolled pairing of original chèvre with tart cranberries and warm cinnamon.
- **Fig**, a classic combo of goat chèvre infused with premium Dalmatian figs.
- **Original Plain Goat Cheese Log**, exceptionally smooth, slightly acidic but fresh tasting.

....

The hand-formed triangular prism shape with a black ash mixed rind distinguishes this eye-catching goat cheese from the beginning. Enjoy the well-rounded yet complex flavours early in the life of this cheese, or try it near the expiration date, when it is boldly caprine, acidic and slightly peppery, like the famous Loire goat cheeses of France. Cendrillon (pronounced *san-dree-yown*) was crowned "World Champion" out of nearly 2,500 cheeses at the World Cheese Competition in 2009. The name means "Cinderella" and it is made by Alexis de Portneuf, the fine cheese division of Saputo—proving that big companies can make excellent artisan-style specialty cheese even though the process may be on a large scale.

Cendrillon

Fromagerie Alexis de Portneuf
Saint-Raymond-de-Portneuf, QC

Fromagerie
Alexis de Portneuf

Tasting Notes

C'estbon Chèvre

C'estbon Cheese
St. Marys, ON

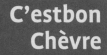

One of the first farmstead goat milk cheese artisans in Ontario, George Taylor turned a family hobby into a business, but he still packs his product in little white cups with a distinctive blue label. For me it remains the *crème de la crème* of chèvre for its consistency, with clean flavour and a fluffy, light texture—the result of time-consuming hand-ladling of the fresh coagulated curd into draining bags.

Champagnole

Fromagerie Chaput
Châteauguay, QC

The Chaput family is masterful in their raw goat milk cheese creations. This firm washed rind with a vegetal ochre-coloured crust is carefully aged six months to develop the specific character of the cheese. The fragrant aroma prepares the taste buds for several layers of flavour, from salty and grassy to lemon to hazelnut.

Chèvre à ma Manière

Fromagerie l'Atelier
Ste-Hélène-de-Chester, QC

I've said it before, and with this cheese I'll say it again: Canada has some extraordinary goat-milk cheese producers. Their products have the sophistication in appearance, aroma and flavour to transport you right to the Loire region in France. But why go there when a cheese like Ma Manière (meaning "my way") is available right here in Quebec?

This masterpiece in fromage is made by Simon Hamel and produced under the brand Fromagerie l'Atelier at La Moutonnière, where he also does cheesemaking. Formed into a thin disk weighing 300 grams, the silky paste of this soft, lactic ripened cheese is encased in a wrinkly geotrichum rind that is known to have colourful little moulds growing on it. The delicate aroma and ensuing tastes are similar: straw, butter, fresh caprine milk. Tangy and fresh, all in the same bite!

This is the 100% goat version of Empereur (see page 110). Try them side by side to fully appreciate the effect of changing the type of milk on basically the same cheese. Chevrochon is a soft washed rind, silkier in texture and lighter in taste than its cow-milk cousin, but still possessing an earthy aroma from the bacteria used to wash the cheese. I really like them both, with a slight preference for Chevrochon because there are so few washed rind goat cheeses.

Chevrochon
Fromagerie Fritz Kaiser
Noyan, QC

Cheese FAQ:
Why is some cheese seasonal?

Best Baa Farms

There are two major reasons for "seasonal" cheese. First, in the natural order of the world, sheep lactate (produce milk) after birthing for only five to eight months, while goats lactate for about eight months (depending on the breed). There are ways to "force" milk from the animal (lengthen the lactation cycle) for additional months, typically by lighting the barn during dark times of the day, but this destroys the animal's natural rhythms and stresses it. Most artisans respect and care for their animals enough to give them a break. If there is surplus milk during milking season, sheep milk can be frozen for cheesemaking in the winter. Surplus goat milk can be frozen, but more often it is first made into curd and then frozen. The goal of cheesemakers is to make all their cheese with fresh milk, varying the style of cheese to suit milk availability. Firmer cheeses require more milk and thus are made in summer, to ripen for selling and/or consuming in winter.

The second reason for seasonal cheesemaking is pasturing for cows and sheep. When animals eat fresh field salads of greens and can roam outside for long hours, both milk quality and the flavour of the cheese are influenced positively. These attributes greatly affect the finished cheese. In Europe, *d'alpage*—cheese made from summer mountain milk—is sold at a premium because of its incredible complexity of flavour. It's no wonder cheesemakers opt to only make certain styles of cheese when the animal is in pasture, especially Alpine-style cheeses.

When young (one or two months), this soft lactic ferment, mould ripened goat cheese, formed into a little mound format, has delicate citrus nuances entwined with a fresh chèvre taste. It is quite lovely. However, at three to four months Florette is a different cheese, quite acidulous—a love-it-or-hate-it flavour that is too pungent for many caseophiles—tangy, complex and sharp, without any disturbing metallic or dirty afternotes. Florette is right on track for her age and lactic style. I confess to not eating the rind but loving the paste of this four-month cheese of character!

Florette

The Farm House Natural Cheeses
Agassiz, BC

The Smits family think of cheese as a living, breathing piece of geography on which even the water and soil have an effect, a true product of the land—a very accurate statement from this small family-owned and operated farm whose Holstein and Brown Swiss cows provide the milk for most of the cheese they make. The cheese I especially enjoy from their lineup is the farmstead Goat Gouda, which, like farmstead cow Gouda, is amazingly different from large-scale production goat Gouda. Three coats of a yellow waxy exterior are used to protect this mild to medium aged cheese, providing a striking contrast to the dense, pure white pasteurized goat milk paste. The aroma

Goat Gouda

Smits & Co.w Farm Cheese
Chilliwack, BC

and tastes match: clean and balanced, slightly tangy goat essence and a bare hint of caramel. Goat Gouda is available in several spiced varieties too.

Grey Owl

Fromagerie Le Détour
Notre-Dame-du-Lac, QC

Fresh chèvre lovers, rejoice! This is your next step in goat milk cheese appreciation. Featuring soft, dense and luxuriously smooth white curd veiled in a dark grey speckled vegetable ash rind, it is handcrafted in the style of classic French Loire goat cheeses. The flavours are impeccably fresh and incredibly complex, complementing a pleasant lemony tart finish. As it ages, a creamy translucent layer develops beneath the rind. The name Grey Owl commemorates the memory of a beloved eccentric early environmentalist who lived in the 1920s on the shores of Lake Témiscouata, not far from the cheese plant.

Juliette

Salt Spring Island Cheese
Salt Spring Island, BC

David Wood, proprietor of Salt Spring Island Cheese, moved from Toronto and began making cheese in 1994. His simple belief was that a better kind of food business is one that reflects both good community and good food, as the two frequently go together.

Designed to resemble goat milk Camembert, Juliette has a very thin crust compared to cow Camembert; it is the same base cheese as Blue Juliette, without the dusting of blue mould. This pasteurized goat milk cheese has delicate lactic caprine and mushroom flavours that strengthen within just a few weeks of additional aging while the paste softens. Ideally you should eat soft cheeses within a few days of buying them. Unwrapping the cheese and putting it in a plastic tub (with some air) at home allows it to breathe and fends off any bitterness.

Kabritt

**The Farm House
Natural Cheeses**
Agassiz, BC

Available only at the factory store, this semi-firm goat milk cheese is designed not for the Canadian market but rather as part of an initiative to reintroduce goats and cheesemaking to impoverished rural areas in Haiti. Partially funded by an annual fundraiser in Agassiz, the Haiti Goat Project involves teaching people to raise goats for milk and to feed them so they produce more milk, for drinking and for cheesemaking. Of course the cheese will take on its own personality when made in Haiti, but Canadian Kabritt (which means "goat" in Haitian Creole) is pleasingly dry and savoury, with notes of rye or blue in the curd. You can read more about the project and how to help at http://www.farmhousecheeses.com/haiti-goat-project.

Tasting Notes

Lindsay Bandaged Goat Cheddar

Mariposa Dairy
Lindsay, ON

This pasteurized 100% goat milk Cheddar made in the traditional bandaged manner, is astonishing at only 12 to 18 months of age, exhibiting a delightfully earthy caprine milk aroma, with crystals and some crumbliness in the otherwise smooth texture. Flavours are savoury with nutty, lemon/citrus and even caramel overtones, very complex and lingering. This distinctive format for goat Cheddar shows again how bandaged and block formats of Cheddar are quite different. Try the comparison for yourself!

Paillot de Chèvre

Fromagerie Alexis de Portneuf
Saint-Raymond-de-Portneuf, QC

MAPAQ

An excellent and durable clone of French Sainte-Maure, this cheese (pronounced *py-oh duh shev*) is distinguished by plastic straws wrapped around the log of pasteurized goat cheese to protect the bloomy rind and allow air circulation (the original Sainte-Maure has a piece of straw or a stick inserted through its centre). When cut crosswise, concentric circles demonstrate the ripeness of the cheese, with the chalky centre becoming somewhat smaller as the cheese matures. The paste starts its life pure white and fresh, like all goat cheese; ivory tones and more piquant flavour increase with age (three to four weeks). When this cheese becomes grey, it is likely beyond *à point*, with a very acidic taste. Consistently balanced citrus and acidic goat flavours are noteworthy in Paillot.

Canadian Cheese

Pyramide

**The Farm House
Natural Cheeses**
Agassiz, BC

The secret is out: there's no need to travel to the Loire Valley for stunning goat cheese! This small lactic ferment cheese has a squat pyramid format like French Valençay, but it is doused in black vegetable ash for both decorative effect and to slow down the ripening. Pyramide has a very similar flavour profile to Valençay, with a moist, dense, melting paste and complex but not aggressive animal and grass flavours, with a hint of pepper on the finish. When à point, the slightly chalky interior paste is outlined by a cream line beneath the white and ash-coloured moulded rind.

I tasted this cheese at the plant with Debra Amrein-Boyes in October 2013. While the cheese paste was lovely, I found that the rind was a bit thick and overwhelmed the overall taste. She told me that a thick rind is a sign of too much humidity in the ripening room. She then had me taste an ideally thin-skinned Pyramide, where the rind complemented the gorgeous paste. Maintaining a constant humidity is often a cheesemaker's challenge. Out-of-doors humidity affects ripening rooms and caves even though they may have thick walls and tightly fitted doors!

Tasting Notes

Romelia

Salt Spring Island Cheese
Salt Spring Island, BC

MAPAQ

This *très petit* (180 grams) wheel of washed rind goat cheese has grassy aromatics; it is the most pungent cheese from this factory. A most memorable cheese, with a pale orange rind encasing the supple, silky pure white paste, it has balanced notes of grass and lemony goat with a slight salty influence of island sea spray. Founder David Wood was one of the first Canadian cheesemakers to advocate fair trade in all aspects of cheese production, practices you normally associate with coffee, tea or chocolate.

Sabot de Blanchette

Fromagerie La Suisse Normande
Saint-Roch-de-l'Achigan, QC

Goat milk for Sabot is from the factory's own herd, which allows better control over the quality of the milk going into the cheese. This handcrafted squat pyramid of 100% pasteurized soft goat cheese has a wrinkly, furry geotrichum rind, under which are layers of satiny cheese ooze and a chalky but smooth white chèvre paste centre. Flavour and aroma match—bright and lemony, with just the right caprine acidity. A beautiful cheese inside and out!

This is the goat milk version of St. John's Cow Fresh (page 38). Being made with goat milk makes it lighter in texture and flavour, with a bright, sweet goat finish. The key in both the cheesemaking and transporting it home is to be gentle with the curd. It is so delicate that jostling breaks the silken body into clumps. Try the cow and goat varieties side by side to see how a difference in animal milk affects a cheese.

St. John's Goat Fresh Cheese

Portuguese Cheese Company
Toronto, ON

One of my all-time Fritz Kaiser favourites, Tomme du Haut-Richelieu is the 100% goat milk equivalent of Noyan (page 122). It too has a washed rind, a supple body and a hay-like aroma. The texture is smooth, with rich goat lactic and sweet nut flavours.

Tomme du Haut-Richelieu

Fromagerie Fritz Kaiser
Noyan, QC

Appendix A:
What to Eat with Cheese

When it comes to accompaniments for cheese, the last verse of "The Farmer in the Dell" ("the cheese stands alone") has it right. I admit to being much more of a caseophile (cheese lover) than a foodie; when I eat cheese, I like to keep things simple and enjoy it straight up. The restaurants and the countries noted for their cheese concur. A fine piece of cheese needs no accompaniment other than maybe whole-some low-salt bread and an appropriate beverage (ideally a fermented one, such as cider, beer or wine).

In particular, when you are learning about cheese, it is best to focus on the nuances of the cheese rather than complicate things with the additional flavour of an accompaniment. People who know their cheese serve it *au naturel*. Cheeseboards in Italy offer arugula and maybe salt-free bread or breadsticks; in Spain, maybe some fresh veggies or membrillo (quince paste) graces the plate; in France, they still don't understand or accept the fruit and cheese combo that North Americans love (fruit often interferes with wine, let alone the cheese).

Accompaniments are usually a way to "cross-sell" additional items at retail or for a chef to make a culinary statement (more chefs serving perfect cheese would be memorable enough for me) or, sadly, to mask inferior cheese. People are allowed to drink wine solo, so why not let cheese "stand alone" too? It's not that accompaniments don't work, it's just that with a perfect cheese, they are a distraction.

Okay, rant aside, there are a few standard accompaniments that I do enjoy and gladly suggest to satisfy the need to have some food with cheese. The key to picking a food accompaniment for cheese is similar to pairing it with wine. Let the accompaniment either contrast or complement the flavours in the cheese.

Accompaniments to Try

- **Arugula** cleanses the palate and brings out the vegetal taste in soft washed rinds.
- **Dark chocolate** or **beets** are divine with soft goat cheese.
- Dark, hearty **nut breads** provide a nice cleanse between cheeses on a plate.
- **Dried fruit** such as dates, dried apricots and dried apples complement "fruity" cheeses such as aged Cheddar and blue.
- Fresh, unctuous **figs** are ecstasy with just about any cheese.
- **Gingersnaps** cut through the fat and provide contrast to bloomy rinds and blue cheese.
- Grated **truffle** on everyday bloomy rinds raises the bar to elegant.
- **Honey** (just a dab) with blue or other salty cheese makes a nice contrast.
- **Roasted nuts** (hazelnuts, cashews, pecans or almonds) go well with nutty washed rinds and firm cheeses.
- **Salumi** (Italian cured meats) and other charcuterie work nicely with firm and hard cheeses.

Accompaniments to Avoid

- **Crackers** (especially salted ones) are a liability, as their crispness interferes with cheese texture and salt masks cheese flavour.
- **Candied, salted** or **seasoned nuts** are very distracting from the cheese experience.

- **Grapes** will make the wine you drink with cheese taste astringent.
- Most prepared **chutneys** and **jams** are so loaded with salt and spice that the cheese gets lost, even if the jar says they're made to go with cheese.

Cheese as an Accompaniment

As much as I am not a fan of accompaniments *with* cheese, I really like to serve cheese as an accompaniment, just like it is done in Europe. Try a nice portion of cheese alongside a salad, a bowl of soup or a serving of roasted, steamed or braised vegetables, or with a main course that contains the same cheese.

Appendix B: The Significance of Moisture Level

Natural cheese is grouped by moisture level and/or degree of hardness. This affects the ability of a cheese to ripen (age) to perfection, and its cheese "life"—how long it can be stored before quality is affected.

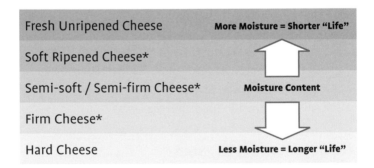

Fresh Unripened Cheese	**More Moisture = Shorter "Life"**
Soft Ripened Cheese*	
Semi-soft / Semi-firm Cheese*	**Moisture Content**
Firm Cheese*	
Hard Cheese	**Less Moisture = Longer "Life"**

* includes washed rind, blue and goat cheeses in this family

Appendix C: Canadian Cheese by Family and Milk Type

Here is an interesting look at which types of cheese are made with which milk. A key to making a good cheese is to know what your milk is best suited for. Thus you will see that some cheese families contain no or few goat or sheep milk cheeses.

Fresh Unripened Cheese

Cow Milk
Bocconcini
Fresh Mozzarella (Fior di Latte, Mozzarina Mediterraneo)
Grey Rush Cream Cheese Style
Guernsey Girl
Halloumi
Labneh
Nabulsi
Noddini
Paneer
  • Malai
  • Tazza Swad Mazedar
Quark
Queso
  • Duro
  • Fresco
  • Paisa
  • Panela
  • Puro Mexicano
Ricotta
St. John's Cow Fresh
Stracchino
Treccia
Tuma
Twist

Goat Milk
Celebrity Chevre
  • Cranberry-Cinnamon, Fig, Original Plain
C'estbon Chèvre
Tiras Feta
St. John's Goat Fresh

Sheep Milk
Ewenity Feta
Feta Moutonnière

Buffalo Milk
Bocconcini
Fresh Mozzarella

Soft Ripened Cheese

Cow Milk
Albert's Leap
Ash Camembert
Bliss (sheep/cow)
Cendré des Prés
Comox Brie
Evanturel
Farm House Camembert
Figaro
Fleurmier
Gaulois de Portneuf
Lady Jane
Marquis de Témiscouata
Noble
Pizy
Pont Blanc
Riopelle
Soeur Angèle (cow/goat)

Goat Milk
Cendrillon
Chèvre à ma Manière
Florette
Grey Owl
Juliette
Paillot de Chèvre
Pyramide
Sabot de Blanchette
Soeur Angèle (cow/goat)

Sheep Milk
Bliss (sheep/cow)
Brebette
Cabanon
Piacere
Ramembert
Raw Milk Ramembert
Sheep in the Meadow

Semi-soft/Semi-firm Cheese

Cow Milk
Aged Havarti
Boerenkaas
Burrata
Butter Cheese (Le Polichinel)
Flavoured Semi-soft Cheese
  • Black Truffle
  • Madagascar Green Peppercorn
Frère Jacques
Nostralla
São Miguel
Verdelait with Cracked Pepper
Zurigo

Goat Milk
Kabritt

Sheep Milk
Bonnechere
Sein d'Hélène

Washed Rind Cheese

Cow Milk
14 Arpents
1608
Alfred le Fermier
Alpindon
Alpine Gold
Baluchon
Beer Washed Rinds
  • Beau's Beer Washed
  • Le Bocké
  • Fêtard
Canotier de l'Isle
Clandestin (cow/sheep)
Comtomme
Chemin Hatley Road
Curé Labelle
Délice des Appalaches
D'Iberville
Douanier
Empereur
Empereur Light
Fleur-en-Lait
Fou du Roy
Frère Chasseur
Galette
Grand Manitou (cow/sheep/goat)
Gré des Champs
Guillaume Tell
Harvest Moon
Hercule de Charlevoix
Kenogami
L'Artisan Oka
Louis d'Or
Magie du Madawaska
Mamirolle
Mi-Carême
Migneron de Charlevoix
Miranda
Mont-Jacob
Niagara Gold
Noyan
Oka Classique
Oxford's Harvest
Peau Rouge
Pied-de-Vent
Raclette
  • Griffon
  • Compton (Natural and Au Poivre)
  • Little Qualicum
Rang des Îles

Rathtrevor
Secret de Maurice
Tomme de Grosse-Île
Tomme à Rudy
Trappist
Valbert
Victor et Berthold
Wine Washed 1812

Goat Milk
Chevrochon
Grand Manitou (cow/sheep/goat)

Romelia
Tomme du Haut-Richelieu

Sheep Milk
Brigitte
Clandestin (cow/sheep)
Ewenity
Fleur des Monts
Grand Manitou (cow/sheep/goat)
Mouton Rouge
Paradiso
Zacherie Cloutier

Firm Cheese

Cow Milk
Canadian Cheddar
Agropur Grand Cheddar
Avonlea Clothbound Cheddar
Balderson
Farm House Clothbound Cheddar
Cru du Clocher
Curds
 • Squeaky Cheese
Empire Old Fashioned
Flavoured Cheddar
 • Caramelized Onion
 • Maple
 • Thai Curried
Île-aux-Grues
Maple Dale
Organic Cheddar
Perron
Smoked Cheddar
 • Applewood
 • Balderson Double Smoked
 • Maple Smoked Extra Old
Wilton/Jensen

Gouda
Aged Premium Dutch
(Gouda-Style)
Flavoured Gouda
 • Fenugreek
 • Nettle
 • Smoked Onion and Peppercorn
Mini
Aged, Grizzly
Thunder Oak

Provolone
Mezzano Pignata
Sweet

Specialty Firm
Aged Farmhouse
Blackburn
Corvo
Five Brothers
Fleurs d'Ali
Lankaaster
Tomme des Damoiselles
White Grace

Swiss
Organic
Perron
St. Fidèle

Goat Milk
Champagnole
Gouda
Lindsay Bandaged Cheddar

Sheep Milk
Allegretto Abitibi
Eweda
Eweda Cru
Monforte Cheddar

Hard Cheese

Cow Milk
Aged Lankaaster
Aged Pepato
Asiago
Handeck
Old Grizzly

Sheep Milk
Tania Toscana
Toscano

Blue Cheese

Cow Milk
Baby Blue
Bleu Bénédictin
Bleu d'Élizabeth
Celtic Blue
Ciel de Charlevoix
Country Blue
Devil's Rock
Dragon's Breath
Ermite
Geai Bleu

King Cole Blue
Rassembleu
Tiger Blue

Goat Milk
Blue Juliette

Sheep Milk
Le Bleu
Étoile Bleue de Saint-Rémi
Highland Blue

Appendix D: Canadian Cheese by Province and Producer

Alberta

Producer	Cheeses	Website
Foothills Cheese, Didsbury	Rocky Mountain Quark	www.foothillscreamery.com
Latin Foods, Calgary	Queso Duro, Queso Fresco, Queso Paisa	www.fresk-o.com
Sylvan Star Cheese Ltd., Red Deer	Aged Gouda, Grizzly, Old Grizzly	www.sylvanstarcheesefarm.ca
Tiras Dairies, Camrose	Tiras Goat Feta	www.tiras.ca

British Columbia

Producer	Cheeses	Website
Golden Ears Cheesecrafters, Maple Ridge	Aged Havarti	www.cheesecrafters.ca
Kootenay Alpine Cheese, Creston	Alpindon, Nostralla	www.kootenayalpinecheese.com
Little Qualicum Cheeseworks, Parkville	Raclette, Rathtrevor	www.cheeseworks.ca
Moonstruck Organic Cheese, Salt Spring Island	Ash Camembert, Baby Blue, White Grace	www.moonstruckcheese.com
Natural Pastures Cheese, Courtenay	Aged Farmhouse, Boerenkaas, Comox Brie, Mozzarella di Bufala, Verdelait (Cracked Pepper)	www.naturalpastures.com
Poplar Grove Cheese, Penticton	Harvest Moon, Tiger Blue	www.poplargrovecheese.ca
Salt Spring Island Cheese Company, Salt Spring Island	Blue Juliette, Juliette, Romelia	www.saltspringcheese.com
Smits & Co.w Farm Cheese, Chilliwack	Goat Gouda	www.smitsandcow.com
Squeaky Cheese, Armstrong	Cheddar Curds	www.squeakycheese.ca
The Farm House Natural Cheeses, Agassiz	Clothbound Cheddar, Alpine Gold, Country Blue, Farm House Camembert, Florette, Kabritt, Lady Jane, Pyramid, Quark	www.farmhousecheeses.com
Upper Bench Winery and Creamery, Pentiction	King Cole Blue	www.upperbench.ca/cheese

Manitoba

Producer	Cheeses	Website
Bothwell Cheese Inc., New Bothwell	Black Truffle Cheese, Madagascar Green Peppercorn Cheese, Maple Smoked Extra Old Cheddar	www.bothwellcheese.com
Our Lady of the Prairies Abbey, Holland	Trappist	

New Brunswick

Producer	Cheeses	Website
Armadale Farm Dairy, Roachville	Quark	www.facebook.com/ArmadaleFarmDairyProducts
Bergerie aux Quatre Vents, Sainte-Marie-de-Kent	Geai Bleu	

Nova Scotia

Producer	Cheeses	Website
That Dutchman's Farm, Upper Economy	Dragon's Breath, Mini Gouda	www.denhoek.ca

Ontario

Producer	Cheeses	Website
Back Forty Artisan Cheese, Lanark	Bonnechere, Highland Blue	www.artisancheese.ca
Balderson Cheese Company, Winchester	Balderson Cheddar, Double Smoked Cheddar	www.cheese.ca
Best Baa Dairy, Fergus	Brebette, Brigitte, Eweda, Eweda Cru, Ewenity, Feta, Mouton Rouge, Ramembert, Raw Milk Ramembert, Sheep in the Meadow	www.bestbaa.com

Producer	Cheeses	Website
Black River Cheese, Milford	Maple Cheddar	www.blackrivercheese.com
C'estbon Cheese Ltd., St. Marys	C'estbon Chèvre	www.cestboncheese.com
Empire Cheese and Butter Co-op, Campbellford	Empire Old Fashioned Cheddar	www.empirecheese.ca
Glengarry Fine Cheese, Lancaster	Aged Lankaaster, Celtic Blue, Figaro, Fleur en Lait, Lankaaster	www.glengaryfinecheese.com
Grandpa's Dairy Produce, London	Queso Panela, Queso Puro Mexicano	
Gunn's Hill Artisan Cheese, Woodstock	Beau's Beer Washed, Five Brothers, Handeck, Oxford's Harvest, Wine Washed 1812	www.gunnshillcheese.ca
International Cheese, Toronto	Aged Pepato, Bocconcini, Fior di Latte, Noddini, Provolone Mezzano Pignata, Ricotta, Sweet Provolone, Treccia, Tuma	www.internationalcheese.ca
Local Dairy, Ingersoll	Malai Paneer, Tazza Swad Mazedar	www.localdairy.ca
Maple Dale Cheese, Plainfield	Cheddar	www.mapledalecheese.com
Mariposa Dairy, Lindsay	Celebrity Chevre (Cranberry-Cinnamon, Fig, Original Plain), Lindsay Bandaged Goat Cheddar, Tania Toscana Sheep Milk Cheese	www.mariposadairy.ca
Monforte Dairy, Stratford	Bliss, Monforte Cheddar, Paradiso, Piacere, Toscano	www.monfortedairy.com
Mountainoak Cheese, New Hamburg	Aged Farmhouse Premium Dutch	www.mountainoakcheese.ca
Organic Meadow Cheese, Dundalk	Organic Cheddar	www.organicmeadow.com

Producer	Cheeses	Website
Pine River Cheese and Butter Co-op, Ripley	Caramelized Onion Cheddar, Thai Curried Cheddar, Chocolate Cheese	www.pinerivercheese.com
Portuguese Cheese Company, Toronto	Corvo, São Miguel, St. John's Cow Fresh, St. John's Goat Fresh	www.portuguesecheese.com
Primeridge Pure, Markdale	Grey Rush	www.primeridgepure.ca
Quality Cheese, Vaughan	Albert's Leap, Buffalo and Cow Milk Bocconcini, Burrata, Fresh Cow Milk Mozzarella, Fresh Buffalo Milk Mozzarella, Ricotta, Stracchino	www.qualitycheese.com
Thornloe Cheese, Thornloe	Asiago, Devil's Rock, Evanturel	www.thornloecheese.ca
Thunder Oak Cheese Farm, Thunder Bay	Fenugreek Gouda, Nettle Gouda, Thunder Oak Gouda	www.cheesefarm.ca
Upper Canada Cheese, Jordan Station	Guernsey Curds, Guernsey Girl, Niagara Gold	www.uppercanadacheese.com
Wilton Cheese Factory, Wilton	Jensen Cheddar, Wilton Cheddar	www.jensencheese.ca, www.wiltoncheese.com

Prince Edward Island

Producer	Cheeses	Website
Cows Creamery, Charlottetown	Applewood Smoked Cheddar, Avonlea Clothbound Cheddar	www.cows.ca
Island Farmhouse Gouda/Cheese Lady's Gouda, North Winsloe	Smoked Onion and Peppercorn Gouda	www.peiflavours.ca

Quebec

Producer	Cheeses	Website
Abbaye Saint-Benoît, Saint-Benoît-du-Lac	Bleu Bénédictin, Ermite, Frère Jacques	www.st-benoit-du-lac.com
Agropur Fine Cheese, Longueuil	Agropur Grand Cheddar, L'Artisan Oka, Oka Classique	www.pleasureandcheeses.ca, www.grandcheddar.ca
Au Gré des Champs, Saint-Jean-sur-Richelieu	D'Iberville, Frère Chasseur, Gré des Champs, Pont Blanc	www.augredeschamps.com
Les Dépendances, St-Hubert	Peau Rouge	www.lesdependances.com
Ferme Ducrêt, Saint-Basile-de-Portneuf	Gaulois de Portneuf, Tomme à Rudy	
Fromage au Village, Lorrainville	Cru du Clocher Cheddar, Fleurs d'Ail	www.fromagesduquebec.qc.ca
Fromagerie Alexis de Portneuf, Saint-Raymond-de-Portneuf	Cendrillon, Paillot de Chèvre	www.alexisdeportneuf.com
Fromagerie l'Ancêtre, Bécancour	Organic Cheddar	www.fromagerieancetre.com
Fromagerie l'Atelier, Ste-Hélène-de-Chester	Chèvre à ma Manière	
Fromagerie Blackburn, Jonquière	Blackburn, Mont-Jacob	www.fromagerieblackburn.com
Fromagerie Champêtre, Repentigny	Le Bocké	www.fromageriechampetre.com
Fromagerie Chaput, Châteauguay	Champagnole	www.chaputcheese.com
Fromagerie Le Détour, Notre-Dame-du-Lac	Clandestin, Grey Owl, Magie du Madawaska, Marquis de Témiscouata	www.fromagerieledetour.ca
Fromagerie Domaine Féodal, Berthierville	Cendré des Prés, Guillaume Tell, Noble	www.fromageriedomainefeodal.com
Fromagerie du Charme, Saint-Remi-de-Tingwick	Étoile Bleue de Saint-Rémi	

Producer	Cheeses	Website
Fromagerie du Champ à la Meule, Notre-Dames-de-Lourdes	Fêtard, Victor et Berthold	www.champalameule.com
Fromagerie du Pied-de-Vent, Havre-aux-Maisons	Pied-de-Vent, Tomme des Demoiselles	www.fromagesduquebec.qc.ca
Fromagerie du Presbytère, Sainte Élizabeth-de-Warwick	Bleu d'Élizabeth, Louis d'Or, Fondue d'Or	www.fromageriedupresbytere.com
Fromagerie Éco-Délices, Plessisville	Délice des Appalaches, Mamirolle	www.ecodelices.com
Fromagerie F.X. Pichet, Sainte-Anne de la Pérade	Baluchon	www.fromageriefxpichet.com
Fromagerie Fritz Kaiser, Noyan	Chevrochon, Douanier, Empereur, Empereur Light, Miranda, Noyan, Raclette Griffon, Soeur-Angèle, Tomme du Haut-Richelieu, Zurigo	www.fkaiser.com
Fromagerie Île-aux-Grues, Isle-aux-Grues	Canotier de l'Isle, Île-aux-Grues Cheddar, Mi-Carême, Riopelle, Tomme de Grosse-Île	www.fromagesileauxgrues.com
Fromagerie Lehmann, Hébertville	Kenogami, Valbert	www.fromagesduquebec.qc.ca
Fromagerie Médard, Saint-Gédéon	14 Arpents, Rang des Îles	www.fromageriemedard.com
Fromagerie La Moutonnière Inc., Ste-Hélène-de-Chester	Cabanon, Feta Moutonnière, Fleur des Monts, Le Bleu, Sein d'Hélène	www.lamoutonniere.com
Fromagerie Nouvelle France, Racine	Zacharie Cloutier	www.fromagerienouvellefrance.com
Fromagerie Perron, Saint-Prime	Perron Cheddar, Perron Swiss	www.fromagerieperron.com
Fromagerie Polyethnique, Saint-Robert	Halloumi, Labneh, Nabulsi, Twist	www.lebedouin.com

Producer	Cheeses	Website
Fromagerie Le P'tit Train du Nord, Mont-Laurier	Curé Labelle	www.fromagerie ptittraindunord.com
Fromagerie La Station de Compton, Compton	Alfred le Fermier, Comtomme, Raclette de Compton (Natural and Poivre), Chemin Hatley Road	www. fromagerielastation. com
Fromagerie St-Fidèle, La Malbaie	St. Fidèle Swiss	www.fromageriestfidele. net
Fromagerie La Suisse Normande, Saint-Roch-de-l'Achigan	Grand Manitou, Pizy, Sabot de Blanchette	www.lasuissenormande. com
Fromagerie La Vache à Maillotte, La Sarre	Allegretto Abitibi	vacheamaillotte.com
Les Fromagiers de la Table Ronde, Sainte-Sophie	Fou du Roy, Galette, Rassembleu	www.fromagiers delatableronde.com
Gattuso, Montreal	biobio Organic Cheddar	www.biobio.ca
Laiterie Charlevoix, Baie Saint-Paul	1608 de Charlevoix, Fleurmier, Hercule de Charlevoix	www. fromagescharlevoix. com, www.vachecanadienne. com (Canadienne cow project)
Laiterie Charlifoux, Sorel-Tracy	Butter Cheese (Le Polichinel)	www.fromagersriviera. com
Maison d'Affinage Maurice Dufour, Baie-St-Paul	Ciel de Charlevoix, Migneron, Secret de Maurice	www.fromagefin.com
Saputo, Montreal	Mozzarina Mediterraneo	www.saputo.ca/ OurCheeses

INDEX

This book is an excellent resource for anyone interested in discovering [Canadian] cheeses. I highly recommend this book for anyone wanting to learn more about cheese and have a handy guide to the ... varieties that we may overlook when at the markets
—Spotlight Toronto

Most gourmands have no idea what they're missing in Canadian cheese and yet new Canadian cheeses continue to emerge. In this completely revised and updated edition of a cheese-lover's classic, *Canadian Cheese: A Guide* is a reference to some of the newest, best and most popular cheese.

Sections, content and photographs include:
- Concise tasting notes for 225 artisan cheeses from coast to coast
- What's on your cheese board? Canadian cheese professionals share their favourites
- Wine and beer pairing suggestions
- Tasting notes for Old World cheeses that have influenced New World Canadian styles
- Cheese ladder of appreciation suggestions: if you like this cheese ... try this one
- How to taste cheese like a pro
- Author and cheesemaker anecdotes
- Useful information on buying and serving cheese.

MIX
Paper from responsible sources
FSC® C016245
www.fsc.org

A FIREFLY BOOK

ISBN-13: 978-1-77085-362-1
ISBN-10: 1-77085-362-6

01995

9 781770 853621

Price in U.S. / Canada $19.95
Printed in Canada

Professionally renowned for her work in furthering artisan and specialty cheese in the U.S. and Canada, **Kathy Guidi** founded the first full curriculum cheese appreciation school in North America and is a founding member of the ACS Cheese Professional Certification Program.